Second Chances

Starting Over in the Peace Corps

Denise Sieber

One Printers Way
Altona, MB R0G 0B0
Canada

www.friesenpress.com

Copyright © 2024 by Denise Sieber
First Edition — 2024

All rights reserved.

No part of this publication may be reproduced in any form, or by any means, electronic or mechanical, including photocopying, recording, or any information browsing, storage, or retrieval system, without permission in writing from FriesenPress.

Pseudonyms were used for all people mentioned in my book except for some mentioned by first name only or shown in photos.

ISBN
978-1-03-831839-8 (Hardcover)
978-1-03-831838-1 (Paperback)
978-1-03-831840-4 (eBook)

1. Biography & Autobiography, Personal Memoirs

Distributed to the trade by The Ingram Book Company

TABLE OF CONTENTS

INTRODUCTION	1
CHAPTER 1 Pre-Peace Corps	3
CHAPTER 2 Stateside Training, Colorado	11
CHAPTER 3 In-Country Training *Part 1: Accra* *Part 2: Tamale*	17 17 22
CHAPTER 4 Jirapa	53
CHAPTER 5 Tema	107
AFTERWORD	147
ACKNOWLEDGMENTS	151

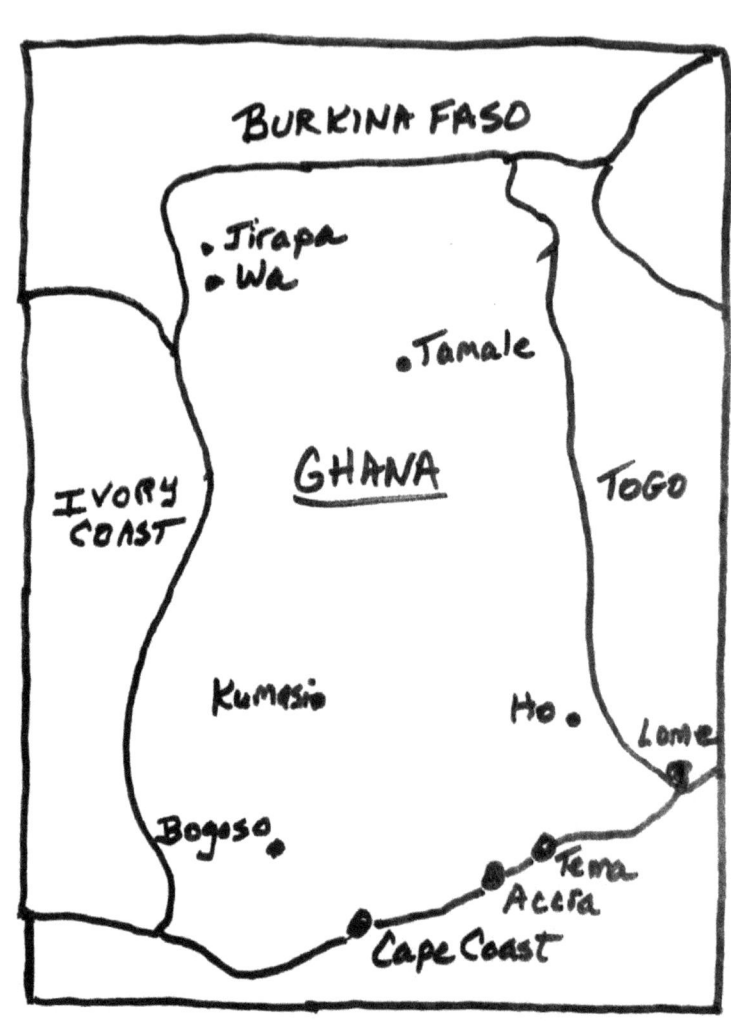

"Vitality shows in not only the ability to persist but the ability to start over."

—F. Scott Fitzgerald

DEDICATION

This is dedicated to my dear mother and friend, Joanne Colbert.

INTRODUCTION

I've been writing this book off and on since the mid-1990s at which time a family friend nudged me to explain why I joined the Peace Corps. "Let them get to know you before taking them on your journey," Marv advised. And so, I did. Excavating early influences that led me to Ghana, West Africa, has been a rewarding journey unto itself.

Flash forward more than a quarter century and here I am on another adventure—this time, in Mexico, where life is once again gloriously slow and simple, in fact, much like Ghana in the mid-1980s. The luxury of time and hindsight that comes with retirement has allowed me to pore over dozens of letters written to my parents from Ghana half a lifetime ago. Handwritten words have greased my memory, rekindling experiences of a young, often immature woman on her first journey far from home.

Mine is a story of risk and redemption, about plunging into the unknown and being rewarded with second chances—the chance to start over, to reinvent one's life by embarking on a journey of self-discovery. It's about overcoming hardship and defying people's expectations, from "you'll never do it" to being voted "most likely to quit." It's about the gifts of learning from other cultures and finishing what you start. It's about how one risk leads to another, each fostering confidence by carving meaning into life. Life, a never-ending book as long as you're willing to look over the wall.

CHAPTER I

Pre-Peace Corps

YOU'LL NEVER DO IT

It was the summer of 1985 when a former college mate unwittingly steered me toward Africa. Diane weaved in and out of her kitchen with armfuls of laundry while I sat on her sofa, eager to tell her about a Peace Corps recruitment event the night before. She continued busying herself with chores, but I pushed on, recounting stories presented by a Peace Corps volunteer who had just returned from two years in Zaire:

"Zairean children gawked whenever they saw a white man coming. Sometimes the adults would taunt the littlest ones, picking them up and thrusting them forward saying, 'Look! It is Father Christmas!' With eyes bulging, the toddlers would grow silent before breaking out into a bloody scream, which of course had all the adults laughing. Oh, and the transportation was unbelievable. During the rainy season, dirt roads turned into muddy obstacle courses with potholes the size of craters. Trucks and cars often got stuck, sometimes days at a time. The cool thing was that strangers always stopped to help each other out. For entertainment, he'd spend evenings stretched out on a hill with his Zaierean friend philosophizing about life under the stars. He said, 'While that probably doesn't sound exciting to those of you who'd prefer to watch a movie on your VCR, this was my idea of fun.'"

Hearing the acronym "VCR" snapped me out of my reverie. It was like stepping on a cold nail. *That's* when I knew I was hooked.

"I've decided," I blurted out to Diane. "I'm joining the Peace Corps. I don't want to be a couch potato watching someone else's adventure. I want my own."

My mind's eye was still gazing up at those stars when I heard her say, "You'll never do it."

Her words stung like a slap in the face, but I wasn't surprised. For too long, I'd been putting up with people who sucked my good energy like ticks hungry for self-esteem. Not this time. This time, I shot back, "Baby, you can drive me to the airport and walk me down the tarmac." Stunned by my own reaction and the angry thumping in my chest, I grabbed my purse and headed for the door, mumbling some lame excuse for leaving.

At the time, all a person had to do was tell me I couldn't do something to push me in that direction. Negative motivation, I'd learned, was a powerful force. After all, meeting yesterday's deadlines and pacifying lawyers' egos for the almighty dollar had long since lost their appeal. In short, I was a burned-out legal secretary with no degree and no direction, only a desperate need to escape my jaded life in Washington, DC.

A MATTER OF WHEN

To fill the void, I had developed a predilection for material things. As my mother used to say, I had "*Iwantitis.*" Then again, that was the 1980s in Northwest, DC, a time when everyone blew tons of money going out to lunch and dinner, and no one batted an eye at dropping $200 for a Brooks Brothers suit, $80 for a hairstyle, and hundreds more for a health club membership.

When material things failed, I found myself caught in a vicious cycle of overeating and starving myself while flitting from one relationship to the next. Eventually, it was clear no one and nothing could cure or conceal the emptiness inside. By the summer of '85, I registered 160 on the scale, signaling the need for drastic change. It was time to discard the artificial for something authentic, something I could call my own.

First, I interviewed for an intelligence job in Canberra, Australia. Then came a rejection for having been too truthful about trying drugs. Then an old dream resurfaced. Those TV ads of Peace Corps volunteers mucking it up in rice paddy fields now seemed a viable alternative to my ill-suited lifestyle. Increasingly, the adventure and challenges of living in a third-world country appealed to me. Yet there I was, twenty-four years old in conservative DC with a circle of friends who would no more leave their hair dryers for a stint in Southeast Asia than would ZsaZsa Gabor. *Do I really have what it takes to go through with this?*

My chances were slim, and I knew it. After all, the application process was highly competitive. Rumor had it, the Peace Corps not only recruited college graduates but favored Ivy Leaguers.

Thanks to my parents, who'd instilled in me a belief in my ability to shine above the rest, I dug down deep and fought the odds. After submitting a painstakingly long application with every conceivable reason they should recruit me (even my love of camping), I decided it wasn't a matter of if but when the Peace Corps offered me a job. In the process, I played the squeaky wheel, attending every recruitment event, making damn sure my name appeared on their attendance lists. Over time, my enthusiasm had grown into unabashed determination, and my recruiter knew it.

THE OFFER

"I have only the weekend to decide?" The official voice on the other end of the phone was unyielding.

"Yes, you have until Monday to accept our offer."

After waiting over a year to hear back from the Peace Corps, I now had only two days to decide whether to spend the next two years of my life in Africa. My heart hammered like a cornered jack rabbit's.

"Where in West Africa?" I asked incredulously.

"Ghana," she repeated.

Suddenly, I was floating far above my desk. After thanking the HR woman, I put down the receiver and stared absently at the ink blotter below me. *Holy crap. They just called my bluff, and I deserve it!*

Like the Grinch's grin on Christmas morning, a slow smile crept up my face. Not knowing whether to laugh, cry, jump, or shout, I sat there frozen, vaguely aware of my feet doing a jig all on their own. Then a rush of adrenaline catapulted me out of my chair. Pacing the hallways, I wondered whether to tell anyone. *Hot damn, so this is what it's like to win the lottery!* As a snotty recruiter later explained it, I "barely got in by the skin of [my] nose due to a more qualified candidate declining [Peace Corps'] offer."

That Sunday, I joined my family in celebration of Mother's Day with all the anticipation of an agitator known for reveling in shock effect. While reluctant to steal my mom's thunder, I knew if I could muster the courage to tell my parents, I'd have the strength to accept Peace Corps' offer that Monday. Grateful for their support, I signed up the next morning for a two-year assignment in Ghana.

THE WHY

Over time, friends and family asked, "Why the Peace Corps? Why not help people in your own country?" There was no easy answer. After all, what makes a person join the Marines versus AmeriCorps? Maybe it takes a combination of one's DNA and early childhood experiences to steer people beyond the comfort of their backyard. All I know is that since my childhood, I've gravitated toward people who look and sound nothing like me.

From my early days, whether playing dolls with Regina, an effervescent Black friend, or competing on the swim team with Laney, a shy Taiwanese friend, people from different cultures have always fascinated me. Coming from a predominantly white, middle-class neighborhood, my childhood was blessed with the absence of negative stereotypes, but it also lacked any real diversity. Regina and Laney were anomalies because of their race, not their socioeconomic class. In spite of this, I rarely saw white adults hanging out with people of color.

Although my parents raised me to value the importance of a person's uniqueness, the notion had all but evaporated by high school, a conformist atmosphere of middle-class kids imitating their rich counterparts on the other side of the tracks, otherwise known as "horse country." Disinclined to join cliques, I, too, had all but evaporated. Then, a kind, soft-spoken boy let me know I counted. What I admired about Ed was his own paradox. On the one hand, he was sensitive and shy; on the other, the quarterback of our high school football team.

One night, after we hit it off at a party, I came home flushed and eager to tell my parents about my new friend. I omitted his status as a popular jock, but they quickly deduced his identity.

"He's the quarterback of the football team, isn't he?" they asked.

"Yes," I replied rather proudly.

7

Then came a long awkward silence, the kind that leaves a knot in the pit of your stomach. *Here it comes. They're going to say something I don't want to hear.* In an effort to protect me, they explained that sometimes Black athletes used white women to elevate their status, especially blondes. Although I respected my parents—they were, after all, an older generation who had lived through different times—I didn't accept their advice to steer clear of him. Instead, every instinct told me Ed appeared on my path for a reason.

As our friendship grew, I resolved to sneak out with him whenever I could. Sneaking around didn't bother me, but I suspect it hurt him on some level. The irony is that it was Ed who elevated my status. The only difference was, I didn't use him, I loved him. After courting during our senior year, we headed off in different directions for college. Eventually, my interest in the other grew into an insatiable desire to understand people from different cultures and the roots of social intolerance. By my mid-twenties, I had dated guys from Lebanon to Uruguay.

But long before then, my parents had planted the seeds, cultivating my curiosity for worlds far beyond our backyard. Piquing my interest at an early age were ever-present stacks of *National Geographic* on our coffee table, a set of encyclopedias lining the living room shelf, and artifacts from my parents' travels sprinkled throughout the house.

As a teenager, Mom had moved with her parents from Japan to Morrocco where she met my father in Casablanca. Soon thereafter, they married in the States, and Dad began traveling extensively for his job. Often, he'd return with exotic gifts and mementos—Spanish castanets, Bahamian music, and a mounted piranha from Brazil. When he wasn't scarce, he was often gruff with a short fuse, intimidating the hell out of my siblings and me whenever he tried to help with our studies. The one exception was when he pointed to the world map hanging on our laundry room wall.

A geography and history buff, Dad lit up like the aurora borealis whenever he talked about a country he had visited or some cataclysmic event that had changed the course of history. Only then did I believe him when he said, "Studying can be fun." Through conversations transcending our closely circumscribed life in the suburbs, his enthusiasm spilled over into a world of possibilities for me. At a young age, foreign people and places weren't frightening or hard to imagine; they were fascinating and tangible.

THE SHEDDING

A few months before taking off for the Peace Corps, I put myself in training, physically and mentally. If I was going to make it through the next two years, I knew my body needed to be as lean as my mind keen. I started running religiously, shedding excess weight and makeup while appreciating the people and things I had taken for granted. That was the easy part. Then came the time-consuming, emotionally draining tasks of shedding my belongings and saying goodbye to people near and dear.

After cleaning up shop at the office came parties with colleagues, culminating in a big send-off that my parents threw for me. Surrounded by friends and those of my parents, the evening ended in tearful goodbyes to people I didn't know whether I'd ever see again. Then I sold most of my furniture and Datsun B2-10 after a prospective buyer had managed to destroy the clutch. Liberated from the heavy weight of belongings and bills, I was free for the first time in my life.

Then came a slew of exorbitant expenses, from several doctor appointments required by the Peace Corps to my first pair of prescription glasses and a cotton wardrobe suitable for sub-Saharan weather. Then there was the requisite gear, ranging from Birkenstocks and a Swiss Army knife to a shortwave radio and a duffel bag.

To this day, I still laugh at the memory of my mother and me shoving a two-year supply of tampons called "OBs" into the mouth of my guitar. We laughed hysterically, imagining the suspicious look of a Ghanaian customs officer inspecting my guitar. Exhausted and spent, it didn't take much to push us over the edge. Packed and ready to leave, my emotions had all but dried up, except for one tiny reserve I fiercely protected.

It was my last night in DC, and my best friends, Carol and Jack, were treating me to dinner at a trendy restaurant in Georgetown. Jokingly referred to as "The Last Supper," I savored every morsel of seafood and drop of wine. Afterward, they dropped me off at my parents' car where I turned and thanked them before sprinting to the door.

You can't leave without giving them a hug, I told myself. *Oh yes you can because an embrace will shatter you in a million pieces like Wile E. Coyote at the bottom of a cliff.* With a brief wave, I hit the gas.

By midnight I was standing in my parents' kitchen admiring a parting gift from Carol and Jack—a gold necklace with a cross and a Saint Christopher medallion. Feeling the weight of guilt around my neck, I called them and apologized, saying goodbye the only way I knew how. From a distance.

CHAPTER 2

Stateside Training, Colorado

STARTING OVER

Our six-week training at Alamosa State College in southern Colorado constituted the closest thing to boot camp I had ever experienced. Most days we worked from eight in the morning until ten at night, walking from classes to meetings and writing lesson plans in between. Our days were so regimented, one of the trainees coined our allotted free time "scheduled fun."

I couldn't help but feel the collective eye of our trainers scrutinizing our every move. If we couldn't pass their litmus test, we could always "ET," or early-terminate, whether involuntarily or on our own volition. While demonstrating flexibility was key, it was only one of several less-than-transparent criteria.

As it turned out, our director, a rugged, full-of-himself character, enjoyed feeding on the insecurities of less-resilient types unfamiliar with the rigors of multiple mind trips. Despite an occasional lapse of paranoia, his terror tactics generally rolled off me. Having already immersed myself in one of those exorbitantly expensive self-discovery programs called *Lifespring*, it was clear the cost had finally paid off.

While training was demanding, it was also exhilarating. I delighted in Colorado's vast beauty as I did my newfound anonymity among the trainees, a group as diverse as the many states from which they hailed. From California to Maryland and

Minnesota to Missouri, there were Deadheads, dweebs, granolas, and grandparents. Then there was me, a certifiable city slicker who reeked of everything average.

Eager to meet the challenges of a highly regimented program, I plunged into training, vulnerable yet hungry to succeed. Slowly, I felt an old innocence return as my jaded layers peeled away. No longer did I feel the chains of people's preconceived notions, attachments to my belongings, or the heavy burden of bills. I was finally and truly alive. To this day, no image speaks more clearly of the vitality I felt than the open skies of Colorado.

LEARNING TO TEACH

Microteaching was an effective method the Peace Corps used to train us how to teach. We were each instructed to stand by a chalkboard and teach a mock class of fellow trainees while being videotaped. Afterward, our trainer would play back the video, then open up the floor for constructive criticism. Watching myself in third person, I quickly noticed what I did well and where I faltered, usually in the form of nervous tics like brushing my hair out of my face.

Even more effective was hearing something I'd never heard. Our trainer actually described one of my classes as "exemplary." *Who, me?* I was incredulous. Bolstered by positive feedback, I set out to be the best I could, teaching for the first time at a nearby middle school.

Day one: My students looked nothing like me. They were mostly Hispanic, aloof, and tough, some slouching in their seats, others sporting studded, black leather bracelets. I squirmed self-consciously under my white skin. Having had no experience with Chicanos or Central Americans, it was clear I was up against a steep learning curve.

I questioned my ability to earn their respect and decided to meet with the principal, a veteran educator who had dedicated her life to students for decades. Despite a serious illness, Carmen was deeply devoted to them. I was so inspired by her selfless compassion that I found myself wishing I could get her on *60 Minutes* for the world to learn from her example.

As Carmen explained it, the most important thing I could do for these teens of migrant workers was to expand their realm of possibilities beyond working the fields. School, I learned, was a luxury for migrants who could ill afford to relinquish their kids' time to the classroom. I decided to ditch one of my typing classes and took the students on a field trip to expose them to different professions in their community. Remembering how much I'd been into music at my students' age, I scheduled our first interview with a DJ at a nearby radio station.

After arriving at the station, we headed into a studio where I encouraged the DJ to talk about his job. Several minutes later, one of my students raised his hand to ask a question; then two more followed suit. From there, we walked to another local business and returned to Alamosa State College to meet with the admissions officer. Exposing my students to different ways of earning a living gave me a singular joy, the kind that comes from opening a young person's eyes to other possibilities in life.

LIFTOFF

Strange, insistent voices intruded on my sleep as a ray of light penetrated my left temple. "Would you like some coffee?" I heard a stewardess ask. My hand reached out mechanically. *What time was it? Where were we?* I squinted toward the blinding sunrise on my left.

"Good morning, passengers. We have just crossed the Atlantic and will soon be approaching Gatwick Airport. If you look to the north..."

I leaned across my boyfriend, Sam, a volunteer I had met during training, then crooked my neck toward the window. Below was a quilt of emerald, lime, and forest green. Immediately I was smitten. Checking myself, I thought, *Surely, you've seen this view flying over your own country.* The pilot then came back on the intercom announcing we were about to land. Suddenly, an alarm went off in my chest followed by internal chatter. *I can't believe I'm here! Am I actually going through with this?*

My father was a thousand miles away, yet still I managed to hear his voice. "*Too late now, kiddo.*"

Since departing Alamosa, Colorado, at six in the morning on August 9, 1986, the Peace Corps trainees and I had been traveling well over twenty hours, first to Denver, then Minneapolis where Prince, the musician, boarded our plane. All eyes were pinned on the small-framed celebrity. It was hard to believe we were looking at a perfectly normal, albeit small man with a handsome face and a large afro, unlike the androgynous, slicked-out image he'd cultivated on stage. The only thing familiar were his three-inch platforms.

Even harder to believe was the distance we'd traveled since celebrating the night before at a Tex-Mex restaurant north of the Rio Grande. Relieved to have survived the rigors of training, we downed margaritas, taking before-photos to compare with after-photos at the end of our service. Meanwhile, we speculated where the Peace Corps might assign us in Ghana.

Although some of the trainees had opted to stay behind in their dorms, no way was I going to miss out on one of the rare occasions we were permitted off campus. Besides, I wanted to surround myself with as many Americans as possible before flying to Ghana. After all, we had forged new bonds once occupied by family and friends. I wasn't about to cut another umbilical cord. Not just yet.

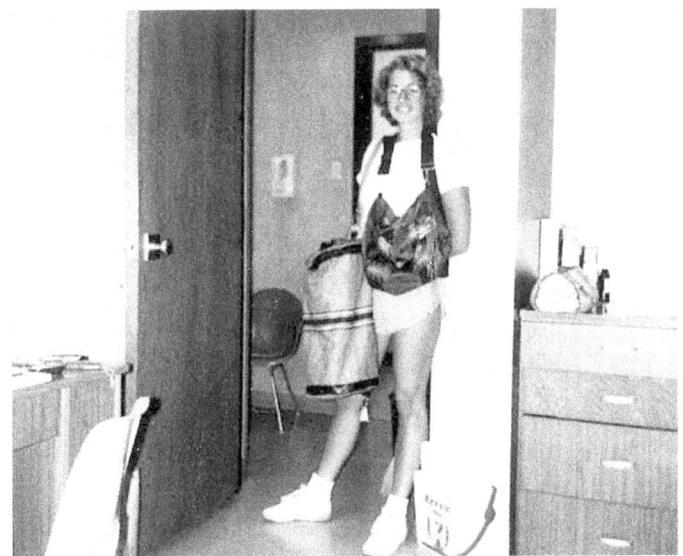

Packing up to leave Alamosa, Colorado

TWILIGHT ZONE

Our shuttle lurched forward, jolting me out of a stupor. I grabbed the nearest pole and pressed my back against a curved wall, attempting to plant my feet, but nothing seemed to be working. The tube was moving so fast I felt like I was being sucked into the Jetson Age at the speed of light. Overcome by the urge to giggle maniacally, I looked around to see if anyone else felt like Rebecca from Sunnybrook Farm on Quaaludes. Unfortunately, everyone was in their own private stupor. We left one twilight zone for another. All twenty Peace Corps trainees and I were suffering from sleep deprivation as we wandered a huge, bustling airport near London.

We were told to stick together, but our heads were barely attached. Had I not been concerned with losing my group or missing my connection, I would have gladly planted myself on a bench, enjoying the parade of foreign faces passing by. The whole time, my ears were jealous of each other, to bastardize my Grandma Mary's expression. I envisioned them looking like two satellite dishes homing in on the multitude of accents and languages.

After arriving at our gate, one of the trainers announced our flight had been delayed by five hours. With a collective moan, we splintered off in different directions. I opted to join a group of women equally interested in finding food. Having no concept of whether it was breakfast, lunch, or dinnertime, I reached for what appeared to be a healthy-looking sandwich with limp alfalfa sprouts dangling from the sides. Later, we met up with the others who were now sitting on the floor by the gate. I pulled out my guitar and strummed awhile, feeling conspicuously like a corny stereotype of a Peace Corps volunteer. Finally, it was time to board the plane.

Next stop: Nigeria.

Black faces bobbed up and down behind rows of blue seats. Most appeared to be African, wearing colorful clothes, headdresses, and white smocks and pants. After settling into my seat, a reflection in the window revealed whites and Blacks scrutinizing each other in a not-so-discreet fashion. Somewhere between England and Nigeria, my left knee locked into a throbbing knot. I got up to walk the aisle several times, but the pain was relentless. With tears streaming down my face, I attempted to remove a pair of glasses that were definitely not sitting on my nose. Defeated, I rested my arms on the seat in front and lowered my head, slipping into a short, blessed sleep. *Note to self: Never wear tight jeans on a long flight.*

CHAPTER 3

In-Country Training
Part 1: Accra

AKWAABA!

It was 9:00 p.m. when our plane descended on the southern coast of Ghana over the capital of Accra. Flat, arid plains surrounded Kotoka Airport, reminding me of a scene out of the TV series *Death Valley*. Suddenly, hushed voices exploded into laughter. Turning my attention toward the commotion, a great white smile was floating in the center of a dark aisle. Nearly as dark was the stout Ghanaian man swinging his arms up and out like a crazed conductor. Somehow, one of our more jovial trainers had persuaded the passengers to sing the Ghanaian national anthem in Twi (pronounced "chwee"). Normally, I would have seized the opportunity to sing, but I couldn't summon the verses. Instead, I lip-synched.

Moments later, the engine silenced, spreading an uneasy calm throughout the cabin. Just then, my heart bucked into my ribs. Once again, I heard my father's voice: *Now there's no turning back—not to the comfort of family and friends nor the luxuries of life in the US.*

For the first time, I felt utterly alone. Snapping out of it, I clutched my straw bag bulging with last-minute hangers and joined the passengers surging toward the exit. We were hobbling

17

down the steps when a barrage of camera flashes assaulted our vision. On the tarmac below, a group of older whites and Africans were greeting us, but I couldn't make out what they were saying.

"*Akwaaba! Akwaaba!*"

To our left was a raucous group of younger whites greeting us from the airport balcony. Dressed in African clothes, beads, and goofy cat glasses, I could only surmise they were Peace Corps volunteers. *God, I hope I don't look like that in two years.* Just then, I remembered what *akwaaba* meant. We were being welcomed in Twi.

Rumor had it the Peace Corps director, Lorette Ruppe, was among the crowd waiting on the tarmac. After all, it was Peace Corps' twenty-fifth anniversary, which was probably why they asked us to walk back up to the plane, rinse, and repeat for another round of photos. Schlepping my stuff up the steps, I lamented to anyone in earshot, "So this is what it feels like to be the president."

Customs turned out to be a breeze, with one exception. As Mom and I had predicted back in Maryland, a male customs officer shook my guitar until the rattling inside caught his attention. He threw me a suspicious look, then took my guitar out of the case, turned it upside down, and started shaking it until out popped a few OBs onto the counter. With a grave air, he picked up one of the tampons and proceeded to examine it. The longer he looked, the harder it was not to laugh. *What was he thinking? Could it be cocaine or some James Bond device?* Finally, a female officer standing next to him whispered in his ear. He looked down, nodding his head, then hastily threw the OBs back into my guitar.

Calmed by much-needed comic relief, I left the airport in search of a Peace Corps van that was supposed to be waiting for us. Just as I started salivating over the thought of a tall, cold beer, a gaggle of Ghanaian boys came running up to me. One grabbed my bag for a *dash*, or a tip, while the others badgered me to carry my bags. Seizing the handle of my human-sized duffel bag, I said no thanks several times before making a beeline for the van. After settling into my seat, the van was abuzz with rumors of a welcome banquet that awaited us at our hotel. Once all twenty-one of us were accounted for, the driver took off for the Star Hotel in Accra, where we'd be staying the next several days.

INDOCTRINATION

The trainees and I were sitting at a long table in a brightly lit, open-air restaurant wondering where the hell our welcome banquet was. After a long wait, I dropped my chin into the palm of my hand and stared at a picked-over plate of dry cookies. The latest rumor was that there wasn't going to be any banquet, yet some of us held out hope that the Peace Corps volunteers at the airport would come to our rescue with a round of beers since we didn't have any of the local currency.

Eventually, a few of them showed up carrying large bottles of beer and started chatting it up with some of the trainees. Soon it became clear no one had any intention of parting with their meager stipend. This was my indoctrination into the downside of Peace Corps life, where rumors and stinginess were the norm more often than the exception.

By that point, all I wanted was to go to bed, but we were still waiting for a trainer to assign us our rooms. To kill time, I counted the hours we'd been traveling, as if that was going to make me feel better. Since departing Alamosa on August 9, we had been on the go for thirty-four hours: from Alamosa to Denver; Denver to Minnesota; Minnesota to England; England to Nigeria; and, finally, Nigeria to Ghana.

At last, a trainer appeared, instructing us to pair off before designating our rooms. Suddenly, the trainees sprang to life, each grabbing a roommate. Once again, I was the odd man out, that once-shy kid who'd just lost another game of musical chairs. *Oh well, solitude will come as a welcome reprieve.* As if sleepwalking, I drifted down a series of dark, Gothic corridors reminding me of *Gone with the Wind* after the Civil War came and ravaged Tara's opulence. Everything was alien—the high ceilings, absence of furniture, louvered windows, and giant burgundy drapes billowing into the halls.

CULTURE SHOCK

While checking in at the front desk, I was told I'd be sharing a room with a total stranger, a Ghanaian nurse. Instead of being greeted by a Ghanaian, a gecko peered down from a wall, looking just as startled as I. The air was so thick my shirt clung to me like a second skin. Eager for a bath, I walked to the tub and turned on the faucet, which produced a loud thump and two drops of water. Cursing, I went back to the front desk where the concierge handed me a heavy bucket of water. This time I surveyed the bathroom more closely. *Where are the towels and toilet paper?* A roll of crinkled pink tissue sat on the toilet, which looked like it had fallen in and been left out to dry. No way was I using that. (Later, I'd learn this was its normal appearance.)

Remembering I had packed a beach towel and a pack of Kleenex, I riffled through my duffel bag only to discover splintered glass and herbs strewn throughout my things. Painstakingly, I picked out the debris, plucked my beach towel and Kleenex, and returned to the bathroom. *Christ, where's the soap?* Once again, I dug through my duffel bag looking for soap which, of course, I had failed to pack. Checking the bathroom one last time, I picked up what looked like a half of an olive-brown bar sitting on the edge of the tub. Taking a whiff, I realized it smelled and looked like the soap we'd made from lard in Alamosa. *Oh well, this will have to do.*

Next, I rationed a piece of Kleenex and wiped down the toilet seat, thinking (in all my naïveté) I was in the land of AIDS. Little did I know, not only could I not contract AIDS from sitting on a toilet, but the odds of infection were far greater swapping spit on Dupont Circle in DC. Finally, I rejoiced over the mere task of relieving myself.

Toothbrush in hand, I wondered how I was supposed to brush my teeth with boiled water, a practice the Peace Corps had ingrained in us during stateside training. *Maybe I can ensure the pitcher of water on the desk is boiled by osmosis.* Resigning myself to the possibility of ingesting nasty parasites, I poured a small amount into my glass, dipped the toothbrush, and wondered what next to do. *Hell, why is everything so complicated?* I shook my head, laughing acerbically. *So, this is the beginning of culture shock.*

* * * * *

Secluded on the outskirts of town, our stay in Accra consisted of medical and protocol briefings, paperwork, and more paperwork. One of the more memorable briefings came from a doctor, who advised us that conditions in Ghana were similar to those in DC a hundred years ago. Built on wetlands in a subtropical zone, the US capital was plagued at the time with malaria, cholera and dysentery.

During our free time, we roamed between the hotel and Peace Corps headquarters where there were ample opportunities to mingle with volunteers and staff. A few of the trainees braved it into the city, but I opted to stay behind. I strayed only once from our insulated world, taking a brief walk along a busy street where fume-spewing trucks and taxis sounded their horns as they whizzed past a gas station with a large sign that read "*PETROL.*" Among Britain's legacies after Ghana gained its independence in 1957 were British terms like "petrol" versus "gas" and pronunciations like "fool" for "fuel," which was always good for a chuckle.

Part 2: Tamale

FEET HIT THE DIRT

After four days in Accra, we boarded a cushy, air-conditioned bus for Tamale (pronounced "Tom-allay"), a large city in north-central Ghana where the second half of our training was about to begin. A few hours into the trip, the paved highway turned into dirt roads making for a bumpy ride throughout the remainder of our twelve-hour journey. Keeping mostly to myself, I watched the tropical flora and concrete buildings in the south transform into arid plains punctuated by occasional trees and mud huts as we entered the interior.

Unlike the exotic images I'd come to expect from *National Geographic*, there were no wild animals nor half-naked people. Nevertheless, I was content to remain behind the comfort of a glass pane that separated me from the hot, gritty reality that would soon be mine. The first time my feet hit the dirt, I learned how to discreetly pee on the side of the road. Squatting low, I used my skirt for cover while keeping alert for the curious eyes of children who enjoyed taunting us with the chant, "*obroni kokoo maachi.*" Evidently, this was their way of greeting white people, referred to as "*obronis.*"

By the time we rolled into Tamale, it was pitch black outside. Along the road was a series of lantern lights casting eerie shadows off of kiosks, hawkers, pedestrians, and rows of shanty-like shops. A while later, we arrived in a wooded area where I could just make out a one-story building reminiscent of a canteen at summer camp. Eager to collect my duffel bag, I jumped off the bus and turned on my flashlight, which by then I'd learned to call a "torch" in British parlance. Just then, a Peace Corps guide called for our attention.

"Listen up: The women's compound is over there, and the men's is over here. Everyone will be sharing a hut with their roommates from Alamosa. After collecting your bags, pair off and we'll meet tomorrow morning at nine o'clock in the mess hall."

Phew, at least that's comforting. No more musical chairs. Nadine, my former roommate, and I got along well. We were two odd-shaped pieces who fit nicely together. She was shy but friendly; I was aloof and gregarious, or so I'd been told. What we both shared was our propensity for silliness.

Minutes later, we found our compound—a circular wall enclosing six small, round huts with thatched roofs. Instantly, my ego was inflated. *Ha! Now I can say I've actually lived in a hut!* We chose one situated on the perimeter of the compound and off-loaded our things in the dark. Shining my torch upward, a bare lightbulb appeared at the center of a cone-shaped roof. Nadine found the switch, and *Presto! Let there be light!* Using ropes and nails, we erected our mosquito nets like pros, then left in search of a bathroom.

Through a grove of trees, we heard female voices in the distance. Squinting my eyes, the silhouettes of three women appeared across a clearing. Soon they vanished into what I could only surmise was an outhouse. Following their path, we entered a primitive structure with a low ceiling and no electricity. For our next challenge, we had to figure out how to hop onto a three-foot-high platform with a torch in one hand and a roll of toilet paper in the other without hitting our heads on the ceiling. I stuck the torch between my teeth and made like a crab, crawling onto the platform while averting my eyes from the others crouched side by side like birds on a wire.

Shining the torch between my feet, I aimed for the hole as my thighs started trembling from exhaustion. "Well, *THIS* is a first!" Nadine blurted out. Just then, the room exploded with laughter. Relieved in more ways than one, we returned to our huts, eager to hit the sack. Curling into a fetal position on my sagging cot, I fell asleep to the sound of distant drumming. That night—no lie—I dreamt I was Jane. As in, "Me Jane, you Tarzan."

HUT LIFE

Sunlight burst through the filmy cocoon surrounding my bed. Birds chirped in Dolby sound, waking me from a deep sleep. I checked my alarm clock and perched myself on the edge of the cot, draping the mosquito net around my shoulders. Looking up at our thatched roof, a smile returned to my face. *Woo-hoo! I'm actually here!*

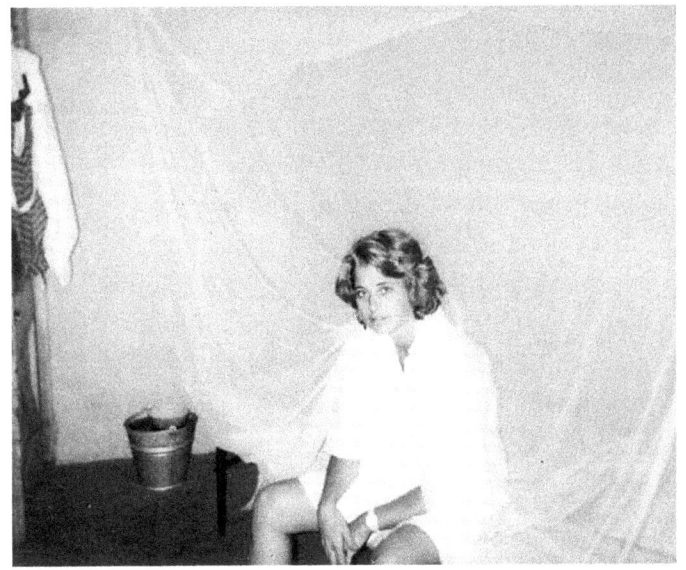

First morning waking up in a hut

Handwashing clothes outside our hut

Our quarters consisted of a concrete floor, a round blue wall, two cots, an old wooden school desk, and a metal chair beneath a window. Our stuff came in twos: two oversized duffel bags, two shortwave radios, two buckets (each), and two calabashes (hollowed-out gourds used for scooping water or, as I'd later learn, serving homemade brew called *pito*). The exception was my lone guitar. Anxious to explore our new surroundings, I opened the door and was greeted by a floral scent on a warm breeze. The compound was still quiet, except for a few hushed voices and some women giggling nearby. Buoyed by my bearings, I set out to perform what used to be a simple task.

Around seven o'clock Nadine and I gathered two buckets each, one for water and the other for carrying a calabash, shampoo, and soap. After wrapping ourselves in beach towels, we headed toward the mess hall to collect water from a rain barrel. Self-conscious of showing too much skin, we smiled at each other, relieved to see other Peace Corps women just as scantily clad. This, after all, was a conservative culture where Ghanaian women didn't even show their knees. Once again, we followed the others' lead across the same clearing as the night before.

Moisture hung heavily in the air, magnifying the hot morning sun, now penetrating my shoulders like a thousand pinpricks. Worse yet, I had filled my bucket with too much water, causing me to stop and switch hands a few times. Soon, an army of black flies began assaulting my eyes, ears, nose, and mouth. Cursing, I swatted at them with my elbows, looking like a demented chicken. The more I flapped, the more my towel threatened to fall as water spilled from my bucket. *Goddamn it!*

I stopped again, tightened my towel, and swatted at the flies with a vengeance this time. Meanwhile, cool Nadine was struggling not to laugh. By the time the shower house appeared, an irrational panic had burrowed under my skin. I picked up the pace, threw open the door, and slammed it shut. Once inside a stall, I put down my buckets and looked up. *Oh shit, no ceiling.* For a few seconds, I held my breath, bracing for an imminent attack. *Phew, all clear.*

Using the calabash, I poured scoopfuls of water over my body, relishing a cold "shower" for the first time in my life—that and its ability to purge the panic from my skin. Lathering my hair with shampoo, I next wondered how it was conceivable to make a bucket of water last long enough to rinse off. Finally, I learned my lesson. Nothing, not one basic ritual, would ever be the same again.

After washing up, we returned to our hut, got dressed, and walked to the mess hall where I devoured a comfortingly familiar breakfast of fried eggs and bread with pineapple jam. Later, I joined a group of trainees who had decided to venture into the market. By word of mouth, we weaved our way through several wooded neighborhoods with single-story homes made of concrete walls and corrugated roofs. *No mud-constructed homes here. Must be a middle-class suburb.* After climbing up a clearing the size of a football field, we stopped to catch our breath. The air was still heavy with moisture, drenching my shirt with sweat.

Then someone said, "Look," pointing to a group of cars parked in the distance. Under the shade of a baobab tree, a dozen or so men leaned against multi-colored Datsuns and white Peugeots. As we'd soon figure out, what we were looking at was a rural transport yard. By the time we got there, I was panting hard, wondering if anyone knew where the hell we were going. Then one of the guys asked a taxi driver if we were headed in the right direction. With a heavy accent, the driver replied, "Just go straight," which sounded more like "stlate," as he pointed to a winding road that disappeared behind a wooded bend. Well, that didn't look straight to me, but I deferred to his sense of direction since I have none.

Twenty minutes later, we came across a trail of Ghanaian women, children, and a few old men walking single file along a tree-lined road next to a deep gutter. Cars and trucks flowed back and forth, liberally sounding their horns, taking me back to hairpin turns along a coastal drive in Jamaica. Some of the women wore vibrant Ghanaian dresses, while others wore a strangely familiar V-neck top with colorful cloths tied around their waists. Those knit tops kept nagging at a distant memory until... *Ah-ha, that's it! Those are the very same tops I wore in the 1970s, when middy skirts and bell bottoms were all the rage.* How strange it was, seeing a fashion that was popular in the States a decade ago.

More striking were the statuesque women balancing massive basins of fruit, wood, and other commodities on their heads supported by erect shoulders and arched backs. As if their burden wasn't enough, many carried babies swaddled to their backs with a cloth tightly wrapped beneath their bobbing heads. I worried for those fragile necks but then checked myself. *Surely, they've been doing this for centuries.* Finally, we reached town.

My first sight was a row of wood-constructed tailor shops; my first whiff, a medley of dried fish, peanut butter, raw meat, and urine-filled gutters baking under the hot sun. Children walked barefoot on littered dirt. People chewed on white sticks hanging from their mouths. (Later, I'd learn that was how they cleaned their teeth). Meanwhile, a cacophony of loud voices in Twi and English vied for my attention from every direction.

After exploring the market an hour or so, my senses had adapted to the onslaught of foreign sights and smells. By the time we returned to our compounds, I felt depleted yet sated by my first real African adventure.

LIVE-INS

After a week in our huts, we were each assigned a Ghanaian family to live with. Referred to as "live-ins," our Ghanaian hosts had volunteered with the Peace Corps to help us assimilate to the language, food, and customs over the five remaining weeks of in-country training. I was matched with a Muslim family of five on the outskirts of campus, far from most of the trainees.

Day one: Several yards ahead loomed my new home, a small, shack-like house with a boarded-up window and a corrugated roof. Once again, I was catapulted back to Jamaica, riding past shantytowns on my way to Negril Beach. It had been my first exposure to abject poverty, filling me with guilt and resentment at once. After all, there I was, going on vacation while countless people lived in jaw-dropping squalor. An inconvenient truth, indeed. *This is payback, girl, big-time.*

I forced my feet toward the front door. After several knocks, a short, plump woman with a round face appeared at the door. Atifa, the mother of the house, smiled timidly, her eyes accentuated by tribal scars on either temple. She seemed puzzled by my extended hand, then shook it limply before showing me my room. Again, a bare light bulb hung from above. Two of her youngest kids, Motari and Sharifa, tagged behind watching my every move.

To my left was a stack of three colorful trunks. The room had neither a dresser nor a closet. *I wonder where they store their belongings? Of course! The trunks.* To the right was a cot next to a school desk and a chair, which I assumed the Peace Corps had loaned them. The only natural light seeped through narrow slits of a boarded-up window. I put my bags down on the cement floor and thanked Atifa, who proceeded to show me the rest of the house.

The foyer, as it turned out, was their main living area furnished with a couch, a hutch, and two straw floor mats. From there, Atifa guided me down a small hallway past the master bedroom, pointing out a dark kitchen before leading me out the back door. Standing on a concrete platform two feet above the ground, I surveyed a small dirt yard enclosed by a brambly fence. Below, several chickens were scratching up dirt; in the distance, two goats were resting by a shed made of sheet metal and dead shrubbery.

To my left a third goat was tethered to the platform near two doors. One was slightly ajar revealing a bucket by a hole in the floor. Inside, the stained walls were the color of Pepto-Bismol. "That is where you wash," Atifa said with a heavy accent. The other door leading to the bathroom was closed. Constructed of chicken wire and a torn sheet of powder-blue vinyl, I wondered if someone had patched the gaping hole with a wad of paper to afford me privacy. Hanging loosely on its hinges, the door became a metaphor for my growing apprehension. Next, we returned to my room where Sharifa was anxious to look at my things.

"Where do the children sleep?" I asked Atifa.

"The boys will stay in the front room and Sharifa with me."

"Oh, I have taken their room?"

Atifa smiled awkwardly, telling me not to worry. I was mortified. This family had given me their children's only room, and I was on the verge of becoming unhinged, just like that powder-blue vinyl door. They had nothing—no toys, no dressers, no beds, nothing. *I will make this work and I will be gracious.*

I lasted five days.

LIONS AND TIGERS AND BEARS, OH MY

Eager for some alone time, Sam and I agreed to meet for a stroll one evening. After dinner, I told Atifa I was going for a walk and headed out the door. Still unfamiliar with the layout of my community, I passed a nearby cornfield and paused, wondering whether to take a path through a wooded area. Eventually, the path led me to the main road toward campus. Twenty minutes later, there was Sam leaning against a tree with that sexy smile.

Surveying our surroundings for curious eyes, we hugged each other, kissing briefly before returning to the main road. Soon, the sky turned dark, giving Sam the license to reach for my hand. (Public displays of affection were a no-no; the exception was same-sex handholding, which struck me as odd since homosexuality was considered a major taboo.) Like a child, I hesitated, afraid of getting caught.

"Don't worry," he assured me. "No one will see us."

I yielded to the warmth of his hand, enjoying the comfort of his physical presence after too many weeks apart. My thoughts drifted back to those nights in the hut listening to an annoying bird as I tried falling asleep. Its song invariably commenced with a *whoop, whoop, whoop,* climaxing into a frenzied staccato, reminding me of the whoopee I wasn't getting. Just then, a fast-approaching car jolted me out of my reverie. Sam yanked my arm so hard I nearly fell into a ditch.

"What did you do that for? He had the whole road to himself!"

"He could've hit us," Sam rebutted. Several moments passed before another set of headlights approached us, from behind this time. Again, Sam jerked my hand toward the edge of the road.

"Damn it! So much for a relaxing walk."

"*Shhhh*," he whispered. "There's someone out there watching us."

Sure enough, behind a row of trees hung a dim lantern at waist level. It wasn't moving. We resumed our walk, intermittently checking through our peripheral vision to see if the lantern was still there. The dim light continued bobbing parallel to our path.

"Oh, to hell with it," I said. "Let's just go back."

Tired and resigned, we returned to campus and stretched out on a picnic table beneath a large tree. Staring silently up at a starless sky, I enjoyed the gentle breeze caressing my skin. Minutes later, the wind picked up, whipping at the leaves overhead.

"Oh shit, I smell rain."

"We'd better get going," Sam warned. "We're going to get dumped on."

I hugged him goodbye and started walking away, but Sam was still following me. I threw him a puzzled look.

"I'll walk you home," he said.

"No, you shouldn't. You're going to get soaked to the bone."

Ever the gallant, he insisted. Now, the winds were whipping at us, signaling an imminent downpour. We picked up our pace and broke into a sprint. By the time Sam and I reached the cornfield near Atifa's house, we were both panting. Just then, the skies unleashed a cold hard rain. We plunged into the cornstalks laughing deliriously like two drunken mice in a maze. Somewhere in the middle, we stopped and caught our breath. Disoriented, I looked around and panicked. Sam must have felt it, too, because just then he yelled, "LIONS AND TIGERS AND BEARS, OH MY!" We burst out laughing all over again.

Finally, in the distance Atifa's porch light appeared.

BEST INTENTIONS

As much as Atifa tried to make me feel comfortable, I struggled to adapt to my living conditions. The electricity was always "broken," forcing me to work by lantern at night with the door closed to keep the kids out. Unfortunately, privacy meant suffocating because my room had no ventilation. The sweat would stream down my arms into puddles on my lesson plans while my eyes grew bleary after a long day of training. The only alternative meant working outside on the front porch, which was out of the question.

Like most children, Atifa's kids were more openly curious than their parents, bolstered by their ability to speak a little English. While at first they'd quietly stare, only occasionally asking questions, it wasn't long before they became as glued to this blonde oddity as Americans are to their TVs. In short, I was their pet goldfish watching magnified eyes follow me around.

Of the three kids, Sharifa was the boldest, perhaps because of her innocence. She had a disarmingly bright smile, big brown eyes, and a brazen demeanor that I found endearing. In turn, she demonstrated her curiosity with no holds barred. When she wasn't following me around and tugging at my attention with her Bambi eyes, she'd sneak into my bedroom to have a look at my things. Farouk was older and well-mannered, but it was the contrast of Sharifa's bright smile and dirty dress that had a way with me. Eventually, I relegated the front porch to letter writing and socializing with the kids.

Posing with Sharifa

Unlike the children, Atifa's husband was rarely around. The only time I saw him was early in the morning when I needed to go to the bathroom. Usually, I'd find him prostrate on a mat in the living room, praying next to his sons sleeping on the sofa. To avoid interrupting him, I'd stand at the edge of the room or go back to bed until he finished. Depending on the urgency, sometimes I'd slip past him while his head was bent down.

Joe ate meals separately from his family, and his family ate separately from me. I figured the male head of the household ate alone because it had something to do with Muslim tradition, but each time Atifa left me alone to eat, I felt more like a guest than part of the family. My mission was to assimilate, yet our interactions were few.

The lack of privacy, ventilation, and interaction with Atifa and her husband were only some of the adjustments I struggled with. Eventually, all the trainees and I had to slow down our internal clocks. The combination of high heat, incredible humidity, strange food, and constant bouts of diarrhea constituted my biggest hurdles. It was purely by default that I replaced a deeply ingrained need to be productive with simply maintaining my health.

After five days of ingesting unboiled water and strange animal parts, my intestines were a mess, exacerbating my already frayed emotional state. It was catch-22 any way you sliced it.

HOSPITALITY'S HAZARDS

In Ghana, where hospitality reigns supreme, you eat what's before you wholeheartedly. In fact, the mere mention of how food smells is frowned upon, even if your intention is to compliment the cook. While Ghanaian hospitality is a wonderful aspect of their culture, it carries its own hazards.

Take, for instance, the day Atifa made me a special meal of *fufu* (pronounced "foofoo"), a sticky starch made of ground cassava or yams and served with groundnut stew, which is essentially a peanut butter sauce with spices, veggies and chicken. A national favorite, fufu is to Ghanaians what mashed potatoes are to Americans, only it has the consistency of Play-Doh. Using your right hand (*never* the left since that's another taboo), you pull a piece of fufu off a sticky blob, press your thumb down in the center, and use it like a ladle to scoop up groundnut stew, which is delicious.

* * * * *

One afternoon, Atifa called out for me from the back porch where she was squatting over two pots and a dead guinea fowl. She turned around and looked up at me with a satisfied smile, uttering only one word: "Watch." I stood behind her as she ripped out the bird's feathers, tore at its skin, and snapped off its legs like two brittle twigs. The entire time I cringed, thinking, *I don't want to watch this.* Instead, I stared vacantly at the floral print on the back of her dress. Moments later, she glanced up at me with sweat rolling down her forehead. I wiped the blank expression from my eyes, replacing it with feigned interest. Atifa then asked me a question in Hausa. This time I was grateful, accepting the challenge to speak her language.

With the bird properly denuded, Atifa began to prepare fufu. She picked up a yam, which looked like a long, tubular potato, then peeled off the skin and boiled it. A while later, she called out for her eldest son, Farouk. Obediently, he appeared and picked up a long wooden staff. Using the entire strength of his upper body, he pounded the yam while Atifa scooped water over it between each crushing blow.

This went on for some time before it occurred to me the water probably wasn't sanitary. I asked Atifa if she had boiled it. Her response was a blank look. Attempting to explain why the Peace Corps had advised us to only consume boiled water, her confusion turned to annoyance. In broken English, she told me that the Peace Corps hadn't instructed her to boil my water. Not wanting to offend Atifa, I felt compelled to eat her fufu that night.

On day five, I pleaded with the Peace Corps to transfer me to another live-in. On top of everything else, I wasn't sleeping well and kept losing weight. They encouraged me to stick it out, explaining that an early departure would cause Atifa and her family to lose face, but I knew I had to put my health first. A day later, the Peace Corps relented, suggesting a workaround.

As a short-term solution, I was allowed to move back into a hut at the compound, which now served as the nurses' quarters, until they could find another family to host me. After resting a few days, Atifa appeared in my doorway. Standing sullenly with tears in her eyes, she asked how I was doing. Her sorrow stung of the offense I had caused. All I could do was assure her that she had been a good host, explaining that my health had brought me there.

AFRYEA TO THE RESCUE

Three days after recuperating at the hut, the Peace Corps assigned me another live-in—a Ghanaian family whose host, Afryea, made it easy to finish out training. Better yet, I was now located in the same community as many of the other trainees, including my boyfriend, Sam.

Like Atifa, Afryea was Muslim but clearly educated. On our first meeting, her robust stature and easy smile exuded a warm strength. Equally comforting was my new environment. I had been given a bright, spacious room with two louvered windows allowing me to work and rest in privacy without suffocating. Although I had stopped hoping for electricity, which was usually "broken" throughout the community, it didn't matter. I enjoyed the glow of lantern light and the gentle breezes easing the dense evening air.

Not only had my physical environment improved, but Afryea, whom I now called "auntie" in deference to the custom of addressing elders in familial terms, provided a variety of healthy meals and deeply missed conversation. A home economics teacher, Afryea was gifted in the kitchen and highly independent. Revealing of her character was the fact that she had named her three-year-old son after her hero, Anwar Sadat, the widely beloved Egyptian president. Sadat had a female twin named Nygat and an older sister whom I rarely saw. Like Atifa, Afryea also spoke Hausa, but it was now much easier to learn the language since she was fluent in English.

After a few days at Afryea's house, I developed an admiration for the discipline with which she began each day. Without fail, Afryea launched into a productive routine in the dark, sometimes well before the chickens. If not the crow of a cock, it was the clinking of pots and pans or the swish of a broom that woke me up. Then came a brief period of silence until, *plop*, the first dollop of donut batter was released into a cauldron of hot oil, producing a loud hiss and a long chain of sizzling. With this morning ritual, there was no need to set my alarm clock.

Often, I'd linger in bed counting the minutes before the first waft of nutmeg floated into my bedroom. While the oil-laden scent sometimes made me nauseous, I rarely refused a few of her fried gems known as *sweetbat*, or what we call donut holes in the States. Some mornings, Afryea would hand me a larger-than-usual portion wrapped in newspaper, saying, "Here is a dash for Sam," with a glint in her eyes.

It soon became evident that Afryea's early-morning production supplemented her income and that of her frequently absent husband. Each morning, she'd send her eldest daughter into the community to sell her sweetbat. After filling a glass case the size of a milk crate, Afryea would place a wrapped cloth on her eldest daughter's head, then the glass case. Balancing it with one hand and her back erect, off she'd go to work.

Through this observation, I learned Ghanaian children provided a valuable source of income and were therefore an important determinant of a woman's marriageability and social status. In the coming years, I'd learn there was no greater curse for a woman than to be barren. As someone who takes pride in her independence and freedom to choose whether to have children, I felt great empathy for these women.

SISTERHOOD

In the tradition of Ghanaian Muslims, Afryea shared her husband with multiple wives, perhaps even mistresses. As I came to learn through conversations with Ghanaians, a woman's social status not only depended on her ability to have children but her attachment to a man, which meant being a mistress yielded greater benefits than abstaining from adultery. This held true for a lot of Ghanaian women, not just Muslims, but it was rarely discussed or openly admitted.

Since Afryea's husband, a well-to-do government official, had his own bungalow in town, our encounters were few and formal. Not long after meeting him one afternoon, my empathy for Afryea grew. While he treated me courteously, he behaved more like a guest than a husband to Afryea. Feeling the bond of sisterhood deepen between us, one night I coaxed her into having a beer with me at a local chop bar despite her concern about drinking alcohol in public. After all, Afryea was Muslim and her husband a bigwig in a town where people talked.

The day after imbibing, I came home from class to find her nursing a black eye. Struggling to conceal my anger, I asked Afryea how this happened. She lowered her eyes and shook her head, unwilling to place blame. My anger turned to guilt. How selfish I was to risk her husband's wrath. This was my first hard lesson in navigating gender relations in Ghana.

NEW LANGUAGE, NEW LESSONS

"*Kin a gin Hausa?*" Kassim asked, pointing to a column of words written on a blackboard at the front of an open-air classroom. The trainees and I sat at small wooden desks under a corrugated roof. It was seven o'clock in the morning, but despite the absence of walls, the room was dark. Without electricity, our only light came from an overcast sky. Straining to see the chalkboard, I was tempted to fall back asleep. Fortunately for me, language came easily. I got a rise out of hearing words like *dundoo* and *talatma* roll off my tongue, much like tasting foreign food for the first time.

Kassim, a young, attractive language instructor with kind eyes, spoke softly as he taught us Hausa, one of the most widely spoken languages in Africa. Yet all I could focus on were the tribal scars fanning out from the corners of his mouth. I wondered what instrument of pain forged those scars, finding myself oddly attracted to a man with cat whiskers.

At that point in training, no one knew where we were going to be assigned once we were sworn in as Peace Corps volunteers. The fact that I'd been instructed to learn Hausa was a good indicator of where I was going to be posted.

Rumor had it that the Peace Corps would be sending me to a remote village in the Upper West region of Ghana. *What is it with me? Do I have a sign plastered to my forehead that reads: I'm flexible, feel free to take advantage?* After all, the Peace Corps knew I was from

DC, and would've adapted almost anywhere . . . except a remote village. I resented that I wasn't learning Twi, the most widely spoken language in Ghana. But something more pressing was gnawing at me.

AMOEBA WALK

Here we go. Once again, my intestines were wreaking havoc. I jumped out of my seat and sprinted across campus, self-consciously clenching my stomach. As soon as my cramps subsided, another round hit me like a ghost punching me out of nowhere. By the time I reached the bathroom, my body was trembling from heat exhaustion, causing my glasses to fog up while I squatted over the toilet. Using my shirt, I wiped off the steam only to discover a mammoth water bug crawling up the bowl between my legs. *Jesus, anything else?*

It was this incident that initiated me into the Twisted Humor Club, which by then the trainees and I had instinctively cultivated as a survival mechanism. After all, resilience required a sick sense of humor; it also brought out the macho in me.

If the men's teasing in my family taught me anything, it was the necessity of deploying a macho attitude in the face of challenges, however stupid the endgame. Discarding my better judgment, I had allowed some veteran volunteers to cajole me into joining them for street chop so I could eat like the locals the other night.

TRIP TO THE RICE LADY

The market was still bustling when we arrived after dark. Weaving our way through crowds and kiosks, one of the volunteers found his favorite chop stand where we stood in a queue of hungry patrons. Increasingly, the foreign sights, sounds, and smells had me wriggling self-consciously under my white skin. Like a child attempting to disappear under a blanket, I convinced myself the dark shielded me from curious eyes.

In the distance, a rowdy group of men were shouting in guttural voices. I turned my attention toward the commotion. Beneath a dim lantern hanging from a tree branch, arms were flying, followed by loud slaps. *Whap, whap, whap!* The shouting intensified. *What the hell?* Squinting, I could just make out a deck of cards splayed across a small table around which the men hovered, their faces gleaming in the dim light. *Wow, this wasn't a fight. It was just a raucous game of cards!* With a great flourish, they slammed their cards on the table, inciting the others to shout in response.

"Yes?" the rice lady asked with sweat rolling down her forehead.

Below her large frame were huge pots of steaming rice, yams, and hunks of meat floating in stew. Off to the right were basins of shredded greens and chopped tomatoes. *God, I miss salads, but dare I?* The Peace Corps had warned us against eating uncooked vegetables due to the risk of parasites. Her wilted look implored me to order.

I asked for rice and mystery meat, then hesitated before ordering lettuce and tomatoes on top. A few minutes later, she presented my meal cradled in a banana leaf. *Oh well, even if I hadn't ordered those veggies, I could still get parasites from that banana leaf.* Without cutlery or napkins, I imitated the others, using four fingers to scoop up my first bite of street chop. Once again, I felt that same rush of bravado the moment I learned I'd be living in a hut.

SAM'S TURN

Not long after moving in with Afryea, I was anxious to hang out with Sam in the privacy of his room. Fortunately, it was now much easier to spend time together since his Ghanaian family's home was adjacent to mine.

One afternoon, we quietly sat on his bed flipping through magazines while listening to tape cassettes on his boom box. I liked his taste in music and our ability to silently spend time together. Occasionally, I'd look up from a page and stare absently at a beam of sunlight stretching across the room. For a moment, I was transported back to a lazy Sunday in the United States. *Ah, the taste of normalcy.*

"Sam, come here," his host commanded. "I have something to show you."

Jacob, the father of his Ghanaian family, was calling out from the front yard through a louvered window above our heads. Sam and I looked at each other, annoyed at the intrusion. Meanwhile, a chicken was squawking from the same direction. Increasingly, the bird grew angry, then frantic. Petrified, we sat frozen in protest. Neither of us had grown up in the country, let alone on a farm, but for the first time we recognized the primal fear of a chicken.

"Sam, come now!"

The chicken was shrieking.

"I'm not going with you," I insisted. "I'm sorry, but I can't watch!"

By this time, the bird's cries were so shrill, I could feel its blood-curdling fear in my bones. I pitied the poor thing, but also Sam. Like the day Atifa told me to watch her tear apart a guinea fowl, it was now Sam's turn to do something against his nature. As for me, I ran across the street and cowered in my bedroom. Despite having closed the door, I could still hear those awful shrieks. Cupping my hands over my ears didn't help either. *God, make it stop.*

Finally, with one blessed blow, came peace.

BOWLING FOR TURD PINS

Unlike listening to the primal fear of a chicken, I developed an appreciation for a peculiar kind of auditory entertainment. Each night, I'd lie awake in bed waiting for the patter of feathery feet to shuffle across the attic floor. Then came the sound of little pellets rolling back and forth. Like clockwork, "Bowling for Turd Pins" commenced at ten o'clock every night. Bemused by my ability to predict this nocturnal ritual, I envisioned a pack of rats knocking around their turds like idle boys kicking stones for the hell of it.

After a brief shuffle came silence. I'd grin to myself, saying, "Let the games begin." Just then, the feathery feet would launch into a mad dash across the ceiling, culminating in raucous thumps against the wall. *Womp, womp . . . womp-womp-womp.* I laughed every time. Aided by a healthy imagination, it didn't take much to amuse myself. Then again, we had other types of visitors that required no imagination.

Sometimes when I came home late at night, I'd have to dodge bats darting up and down the hallway to my bedroom. Eventually, I learned to laugh at that, too. While the novelties of living in Ghana were endless, so too were the opportunities to grow a thick skin.

UNWELCOME GUESTS

Less amusing than darting bats were the tiny red ants that invaded my bedroom whenever I hung my laundry to dry. After hand-washing my bras and underwear in the tub, I'd wring them out and clip them to a rope in the privacy of my bedroom. There were two reasons for this: (1) Ghanaians didn't air their underclothes in public, and (2) hanging laundry outside was an invitation for insects to lay eggs on your clothes which, in turn, could burrow under your skin resulting in tapeworms.

One day while checking to see if my underwear had dried, I discovered a platoon of red ants marching single file down my clothesline. Quickly, I yanked them off the clothespins and started to inspect them. Inside were dozens of tiny ants plastered to the cool, damp fabric. Brushing them off was futile because I'd end up smashing them in the process. There was simply no choice but to rinse and repeat.

After telling Afryea about my quandary, she advised me to hang my underwear beside hers on some twigs concealed by a bush out front. So much for good hygiene. But that was my life, a long series of catch-22s.

GREETINGS, A SHOT OF SEROTONIN

In Ghana, greetings were essential to the fabric of life. Unlike the transient culture of DC, where a stranger's greeting was cause for suspicion, I was now expected to greet and respond to everyone, whether I knew them or not. This, of course, cut against a deeply ingrained code of anonymity. Besides, learning to discern features from a sea of dark faces to which I was unaccustomed would take well more than six weeks of in-country training. Let the *faux pas* begin!

My first glimpse of what to expect came from a litany of greetings in Hausa. In addition to *salam alaikum*, meaning *"peace"* and *"hello,"* there were many other greetings, some of which I found amusing—not only in Hausa but in English as well. Here's a handful spelled phonetically:

Yaya gida = How is your home?
Yaya jiki = How is your body/health?
Ina gajiya = How is your tiredness?

Yaya aiki = How is your work?

Hausa aside, I also learned greetings in Dagbani, the local language in Tamale. This is where things got fun.

The Dagbani greeting for good morning (*naah*) was a great way to start the day. In fact, it was impossible to say *naah*, placing the required nasal emphasis on the "n" with an elongated "ah," without smiling. And since I was definitely *not* a morning person, the spike in serotonin from exchanging smiles was the perfect antidote for early-morning classes. Eventually, greeting people morning, noon, and night helped me break free of my citified armor, connecting me to my new environment.

MODEL SCHOOL TEACHING

Halfway through in-country training, I had grown accustomed to the hot muggy weather, strange food and customs, frequent bouts of diarrhea, and creepy critters. As my acclimation increased, so too did my comfort level teaching at a model school where secondary students came for extra credits during the summer months.

Our trainers assured us these students would be more serious about their studies than their peers during the regular school year, but they seemed reluctant to participate. As a Ghanaian trainer explained it, unlike American kids who are generally uninhibited about raising their hands, the British system discourages Ghanaian students from speaking unless spoken to. My kids were indeed more disciplined than the average American but getting them to raise their hands required a good dose of patience and creativity.

Lesson planning in Tamale

Equally challenging were the poor acoustics in my open-air classrooms. When the kids did speak, they spoke softly with a thick accent, making it difficult to understand them. I could only imagine how hard it was for them to understand me. Since Ghanaians speak British English, not only did they pronounce and spell their words differently, but they enunciated them and never used contractions.

In addition to having to decipher my accent, compounded by my tendency to use contractions, many of the kids seemed distracted by my foreign appearance and mannerisms. Their gazes made me feel more like a sideshow than a teacher, but eventually I grew immune to their curiosity as they, no doubt, grew immune to my foreignness. In the process, I learned to speak slowly, avoiding contractions so they could better understand me.

SECOND CHANCES

THE KEYS AREN'T FUFU!

One day, while teaching typing to my Form 3 class (a younger more challenging set of students), I had had enough of their passive-aggressive behavior. I was failing miserably at instructing them to lightly tap the keys with the tip of their fingers, "lightly" being the operative term. This was their instruction as I called out the keys in home position from left to right:

"A, S, D, F, J, K, L, semicolon."

Instead of tapping the keys, the students smashed them with the flat of their fingers. I felt like a cheerleader growing hoarse from shouting the same thing repeatedly to an unresponsive audience. One day I finally snapped, breaking my rule to never use contractions.

"THE KEYS AREN'T FUFU!" I yelled. "YOU DON'T POUND THEM, YOU TAP THEM!"

The class fell silent, with one exception. In the back of the room, my snarky friend Eleanor, an older business education trainee, blurted out, "BWAHAHAHA!" I don't know who was more shocked, the kids or me. The only thing I could do was glare at her like a parent admonishing a child while trying not to laugh.

LONG-AWAITED NEWS

On the morning of September 11, exactly one month since training began in Tamale, I woke up weary from a record-breaking five trips to the bathroom. It was time to wash up and prepare for my eight-thirty class, but I felt like a sloth. Deducing this latest episode of intestinal havoc was due to my reckless judgment at the rice lady's, I berated myself, knowing the next few days would be jam-packed.

I powered through the morning, passing out my students' final exams, then graded them and tallied their summer term scores later that evening. The following morning, I handed the students their final scores before attending their graduation, a drawn-out series of ceremonial speeches. By midafternoon, I was ready to collapse. But then came long-awaited news. Finally, the Peace Corps announced our site assignments, handing each of us a map of Ghana. I would be living in the village of Jirapa in the Upper West Region, teaching at St. Francis, an all-girl Catholic secondary school.

Scouring the map of Ghana, I searched for Jirapa but nowhere on it was my village. Even worse, only three PCVs were currently living in the region. All were women—one to the north in a village called Nandom; another to the south in a town called Wa; and the third in my village, a nun, of all things. Meanwhile, the previous group of volunteers who'd been living in Tamale hovered around, eager to hear the news. They told me the nun, Sister Sue, was nice and considered the grandma of the group.

They also said Jirapa was about as remote as a village gets. To top it off, the only person from my group assigned to the Upper West was a virtual enigma. Trying to get Brad to open up was like pulling a splinter from your toe. Of all the people in the Upper West, his site was closest to mine. I found myself repeating a deeply ingrained mantra: *I'm flexible, I'm flexible, I'm flexible.* But I knew myself too well. I'd fare far better in a large village, town, or city—any place that appeared on a map.

On the brighter side, I now had an opportunity to teach English as well as typing. Until then, it was anyone's guess whether the Peace Corps needed another English teacher, something I sorely wanted and made a point of asking for. Degree or not, I knew I'd be good at it; besides, the creative challenge of language lessons would offset the monotony of teaching typing. Being the squeaky wheel had paid off once again. Not only did I look forward to teaching English but finally having my own place.

DISCO NIGHT AT PICORNER

Shortly before the end of training, I felt a strange mixture of sadness and excitement all at once. Some of the trainees had also grown melancholy, including Sam, who seemed to be pulling away from me. As it turned out, he and my best friend Robin were assigned to the south—Sam in the village of Bogoso (in the west) and Robin in the village of Akwapim (in the east)—both formidably far from my site.

Around that time, Robin, another PCV named Helen, and I decided to go out dancing at a disco called Picorner with a few Peace Corps guys. Sam refused to go, so I caught a taxi with the girls and met up with the guys at the disco. Knowing this would be one of our last nights together, everyone was in a great mood, talking animatedly as we sat outside at a table having beers. Occasionally, we'd go inside and dance up a storm with Ghanaians and Americans. Among the diverse group on the dance floor were several Germans sporting Rasta hair and funky clothes, even a few same-sex couples letting it all hang out. But then came trouble.

After declining an older Ghanaian man's invitation to dance, he returned to our table, asking me a second time. Again, I declined, politely explaining, "I'm sorry but I'm enjoying our conversation." The third time, he wouldn't take no for an answer. He glared down at me, his stiff body reeking of indignation. Clearly, he wasn't going to back down. All of the sudden, Helen stood up, put her hands on her hips, and said, "Excuse me, but you're being rude. Can't you see we're having a conversation?" *Uh-oh, this could get ugly.*

"In Ghana, you DO as a man ASKS!" he spat at us.

Well, this guy had pushed the wrong button.

"Look at my skin, do I look Ghanaian?" I asked. "Then don't expect me to act like one!" The next thing I knew, he accused us of being racists and stormed back into the disco. We sat there staring at each other in disbelief. A few minutes later, Skip, an older PCV who'd been living in Ghana three years, came up to our table and asked accusatorily, "What did you say to him?" We explained the situation, but Skip was still pissed.

"You don't *do* that in Ghana," he said. "You're *never* supposed to be direct!"

"What do you mean?" I asked, growing more annoyed.

"Tell the guy you've got a headache, anything. Otherwise, it's an insult."

"You've got to be kidding. No one told me I had to lie."

"Do you have any idea of who you were talking to? The man you insulted is the chief of police."

"How was *I* supposed to know?"

By then, all the trainees were abuzz over some commotion inside the disco. Word had it that the chief of police was shutting down the joint. Stupefied, I looked at my friends and said, "No way!" Moments later, the chief stormed outside, announcing he was closing the disco. Sure enough, people started streaming out the door moments before the lights went out.

I never was any good at using my womanly wiles. I guess I'd have to try harder.

IT'S OFFICIAL!

A city slicker pegged by some of the trainees as "most likely to ET," I was proud to make it through training, proving the naysayers wrong. Before becoming an official volunteer at our swearing-in ceremony, the Peace Corps had given each of us an allotment to buy material to have made into a traditional Ghanaian outfit for the ceremony. With *cedis* left over, it was recommended we buy a standard six-foot cloth for traveling, which Ghanaians used for multiple purposes, from a sarong to a shawl. Having come from a country where clothes are ready-made on a rack, it was fun designing an outfit to have custom-made by a tailor. Mine was a striped purple and white tunic with pants and a sash. I also bought a tie-dye cloth, which I still use to this day.

Standing with Sadat outside Afryea's home

In addition to dressing up for the ceremony, we were encouraged to participate in a talent show for which I wrote and performed a song on the guitar. Here's a verse from "The Schisto Song," inspired by Bruce Springsteen and a parasitic disease called *schistosomiasis*:

Well, I've got Schisto in my system, diarrhea galore
Mosquito bites all over my skin, palm oil drippin' out
  my pores
I got three-inch roaches in my toilet bowl, rats rompin' on
  the roof
Little red ants all over the floor, and I think I'm gonna
  jump this coop
Hey-hey, yeah, Hey-hey, yeah . . .

After the festivities, several of us headed over to Tina Base, a favorite watering hole where we'd often talk and debate late into the night. Through these conversations, I learned I could hold my own with far more educated volunteers, instilling in me a newfound confidence, one that would serve me well in the years ahead.

For the time being, it was our last night together, and the mood was somber. I stared at the communal glow of lantern light revealing our tired, sullen faces. All of us seemed lost in thought. After all, the Peace Corps would soon take us to our sites, scattering us across Ghana. Once again, I'd have to embrace the unknown.

CHAPTER 4

Jirapa

ROAD TO PURGATORY

It was an early morning in late September when we departed for our sites. My duffel bag and guitar had been loaded onto the van, and now it was time for goodbyes. Our Ghanaian driver signaled he was ready to leave, but Afryea was nowhere in sight. Fortunately, a sympathetic neighbor came up to me and whispered in my ear, "She is hiding her tears from you."

I struggled with my own emotions, saying goodbye to Sam and Robin, all the while coping with menstrual cramps and knife-like pains emanating from a case of amoebas. This was going to be a very long journey.

Finally, Afryea appeared. We hugged each other long and hard, then I kissed her cheek before boarding the van.

Over rough roads throughout the day, Brad, another volunteer, and I rode crammed in the back on small hard seats surrounded by mounds of luggage. Apart from a few bathroom breaks, our driver was clearly on a mission, stopping only once to drop off the volunteer and twice to hand over large sacks to villagers.

By dusk, we arrived in the Upper West Region when out of nowhere our driver pulled over in a field of tall savannah grass. He hopped out of the van and headed toward the back, inspecting a tire for what seemed like an eternity. Finally, he returned to his seat, announcing we'd have to spend the night in the van until an auto shop opened in the morning.

"What?" I bleated. "No spare?"

A rage-filled rant ignited in my head: *Hell no, I'm not sitting on this brick-hard seat, being attacked by mosquitoes all night!* Simmering at the prospect of getting malaria while trying to sleep upright, I swatted angrily at the incessant buzzing in my ears. Brad and I sat like two slabs of meat at an open-air market attracting swarms of insects. Only there was no air. It was hot and stifling inside. Nor did we have AC, which meant closing the windows was not an option. Weary of swatting at the dark, I pulled out my Ghanaian cloth, covering my arms and head, heat be damned.

It seemed like only a few hours before the driver woke up and turned on the ignition. At daybreak we headed for the tiny village of Tumu near the Burkina Faso border, where I'd heard there were monkeys. I would've loved to see one of my favorite animals in their natural habitat. Instead, we waited for the auto shop to open while fortifying ourselves with bread and coffee diluted with condensed milk. A few hours later, we headed west to Brad's site in the village of Lawra.

Along the way, one of the back doors flew off, landing in a cloud of dust on the road behind us. And just like that, on we went, minus a door. Brad and I threw each other wild-eyed looks, trying hard not to laugh hysterically. Since leaving Tamale the day before, it had been a grueling thirty-two hours by the time we dropped off Brad. A half hour later, we arrived at my site in Jirapa.

Passing through a walled entrance, St. Francis Secondary School consisted of single-story concrete buildings encircling a large dirt field with a smattering of trees here and there. As soon as the driver crossed the field, an elderly white woman flagged his attention, causing him to slow down. Wearing glasses on the tip of her nose and a floppy lime-green hat covered with black flies, she smiled and waved from a distance. Just then, the driver broke the news.

"That is your new housemate, Sister Sue, and here is where you will stay," he said, pointing to a home science building at the back of campus.

"WHAT?"

It was bad enough I had to live and teach at an all-girl Catholic school in a village so remote it's not even on the map. But now the Peace Corps expected me to live with an elderly nun? Surely, they had to know this was hardly optimal. Once again, a familiar rage ignited inside, only this time I spoke up.

"Why didn't you *tell* me I'd be living with her sooner?"

The driver fidgeted in his seat, mumbling some lame excuse. Suddenly, the reality of being sentenced to purgatory for two years came crashing in. *What did I do to deserve this?* Just then, Sister Sue poked her head in the window and greeted us.

"Akwaaba," she said, smiling.

"Hi," I replied, suppressing an emotion universally recognized in Edvard Munch's painting, *The Scream*.

A FAR CRY FROM HOME

Before describing Jirapa, I must provide a disclaimer. Let's face it: At age twenty-six, most of us are still young and dumb, selectively seeing and hearing what we want to see and hear. In other words, our limited experience guided by self-interest prevents us from grasping the big picture.

Compounding my ignorance of a vastly foreign world is the fact that thirty-six years later, here I am trying to recall memories omitted from letters written to my parents. In short, my recollections will not be wholly accurate. With that said, I'll attempt to describe my new environment through the eyes of a twenty-six-year-old.

* * * * *

St. Francis was essentially a metaphorical prison—an island surrounded by bush, crops, cows and goats, and the occasional mud-constructed mosque painted white with wooden poles sticking out like pins in a voodoo doll.

Mosque in the Upper West

Only one road bisected Jirapa leading north to Lawra and south to the city of Wa. I may have had neighbors, but they were concealed by bush and farmland. As far as I could tell, most villagers were dirt poor and illiterate. If I wanted to avoid a two-mile trek to the market, I could walk half a mile to a family-run kiosk where I usually bought cigarettes. Since they never sold an entire pack, I learned to use British parlance, asking for a few "fags" at a time. As for the local language, the villagers spoke Dagari and very little English, rendering my Hausa lessons moot.

The small commercial center of Jirapa consisted of an open-air market, a small hospital, a convent, and a tiny post office, which I had been told was pointless for sending and receiving mail. That was it. You could drive past Jirapa and never know it. This was my new reality. If I was hungry for food or social interaction beyond the walls of St. Francis, I had to walk two miles to the market or wait for a bus.

HAPPY HOUR, JIRAPA STYLE

Not long after arriving in Jirapa, I craved some semblance of what used to be happy hour in DC. Late one afternoon, I decided to head for the market in search of an open-air bar. Eventually, I found three men sitting on a bench drinking tall beers. *Hmmm, looks promising.* I greeted them, then paid for a beer and took a seat. Unfortunately, it was warm, just like the case that Cuthbert, our handyman, had delivered to our flat. Unable to speak Dagari, I stared ahead at a dead goat on top of a wooden table. Its legs protruded obscenely like four wooden sticks, its fur singed by fire.

The next thing I knew, the bar owner sliced open its belly and reached inside, producing an endless strand of intestines like a magician's scarf from a hat. He then wrapped the milky rope around one shoulder and squeezed out the innards into a plastic bowl. *Hmm . . . I wonder what those will be used for.*

Reflecting on what a lawyer once told me, I was grateful to have mastered a poker face since every fiber in me railed against watching the disembowelment of a goat. To avoid the morbid display, my thoughts drifted to my former office mates. Taking a final swig, I smiled sardonically, imagining what they'd have to say about this twist on happy hour.

I was a long way from home, indeed.

THE ART OF WAITING

In Ghana, many girls are named after virtues such as Patience, Prudence and Temperance. There's a reason for that, probably because of women like me who lack in those departments. Soon after arriving at St. Francis, I was handed a lesson in the art of waiting (celibacy was a given). I waited for the students to arrive and for school to begin; I waited for the Peace Corps driver to deliver our mail; I waited for the Tata bus to whisk me away; and I waited for electricity, running water, and cold beer, often to no avail.

The saying "out of sight, out of mind" applied to both the Peace Corps and the Ghanaian government. Evidently, Jirapa was too far out of the way for anyone in the capital to remember us, or so it seemed. Weeks turned into months of rumors that soon we'd receive mail from a Peace Corps driver and funding from the government for the students' food, among other necessities. Meanwhile, no funding meant no food, and no food meant no students. No students, no class, no teaching, no *nada*.

At least my accommodations were cushy by Peace Corps standards: a two-bedroom flat with a spacious living room, kitchen, bathroom, and balcony above the home science classroom. For that, and the orange flamboyant tree in front of our balcony, I was grateful. But much like a prisoner looking down from her castle, I craved contact with the rest of the world.

Flamboyant tree outside our balcony

Sitting in my cushy flat in Jirapa

SINISTER SILENCE

Of all the differences between DC and Jirapa, the most jarring was the absence of sound. Surrounded more by bush than people, the silence was deafening while waiting for the students to arrive. Most days the only thing I heard was the incessant cooing of pigeons or sometimes the screech of a guinea fowl. I've never killed a thing in my life, but there were times I could've taken a BB gun to those pigeons.

Other than managing daily necessities and talking with Sister Sue, the only real activity was the running dialogue inside my head, which often left me feeling unmoored. Fierce hot weather compounded the monotony of life as I watched my stamina slip away. Occasionally, I'd play the guitar, but writing became my true catharsis. Here's a piece I wrote at the time:

> *Temptress of isolation wailing in the wind*
> *Your ghostly fingertips have cast their spell again*
> *Oh, that perverse silence gnawing at my brain*
> *How hot your breath is; thought, movement you disdain*
>
> *My restless habits lie bound beneath your wagging finger*
> *While sardonically you laugh, relentlessly you linger*
>
> *Unwarranted your intrusion remains*
> *Planting seeds of doubt in my captive strength*
> *For though you set with the African sun*
> *Your oppressive silence wavers none*
>
> *My thoughts reverberate, pounding, pounding for an escape*
> *I shall welcome the cool, black blanket of sleep.*

LEARNING THE ROPES

On the bright side, all that waiting allowed ample time to navigate day-to-day necessities before plunging into school—things like getting acquainted with the market, coordinating with Sister Sue's connections to buy jerry cans of kerosene, finding the local incinerator to dump our trash, and pumping water from a borehole, then carrying it home for drinking, bathing, cleaning, and washing clothes.

The water's heavy iron content not only tasted like a rusty nail but often stained my clothes, which I'd have to scrub even harder with soap and knuckles. Fortunately, once the Peace Corps finally delivered mail, my mom was faithful about sending packets of Kool-Aid to drown out the nasty flavor of borehole water. Bad enough we had to drink it warm.

Assimilating was hard but it was also humorous, and humbling.

Before discovering the local incinerator, I learned the hard way never to burn trash on the ground like the locals. One day, I set out to burn a small pile of "rubbish," as they called it, outside our home science building. Minutes later, a gust of wind sent the cinders into a nearby millet field catching it on fire. Terrified, I looked around wild-eyed for help. Fortunately, two Ghanaian women came to my rescue.

To my surprise, they sauntered over, chuckling at the clueless *obroni*, then tamped down the fire with straw mats as if it were nothing. Astonished by their calm demeanor, I thanked them profusely for helping me avert a disaster, one that easily could've torched their food source, as well as my reputation. I may have been a city girl, but I knew in a small village reputation was everything.

I also learned to swallow heartbreaking realities of Ghanaian life in the Upper West. At the market, a handless leper passed me tomatoes using two stumps where her hands used to be.

Crippled men, too poor for a wheelchair, crawled over filthy dirt on all fours. Then came news of horrific accidents on the main road during the dry season.

Harmattan, essentially a six-month drought, brought many tragedies. The hot sun baked the main dirt road where fast-moving trucks, lorries, and buses kicked up clouds of red dust, obscuring the view of oncoming drivers. Crashes killed and maimed throughout the season. The sun was wicked, but so too were the Saharan winds, annually spreading hepatitis and meningitis throughout the village. In a short time, scores of Ghanaians, especially children, succumbed to these devastating diseases. But that's a story for later.

LETTER FROM BOGOSO

One afternoon an older boy came to our flat asking for "Miss Denise." He stood at the doorway, stiff and formal, as if driven by some mysterious mission. *What does this one want now?* I wondered.

Lately, other than Sister Sue, my only contact with humans was with the campus boys who frequently came to our flat offering to bring us water. At first, this made me uneasy. After all, these were African boys offering free labor to white women, which didn't sit well with me. One day I relented, offering to pay them a few *pesewas* (coins) in exchange for two buckets of water. Not only did they refuse payment, but they almost seemed insulted. Finally, I deduced their offers were simply gestures of goodwill, likely prompted by their mothers who were workers housed on campus. After that, I dashed them hard candy in exchange for water, which they gladly accepted. But this older boy, he wasn't interested in offering water.

"You are Miss Denise?" he asked.

"Yes. How can I help you?"

"Master Sam has sent a letter with me."

"Sam?" I asked incredulously.

"Yes," he replied, plucking an envelope from his pocket.

I was astonished. This boy, a student of Sam's, traveled clear across Ghana, going out of his way to deliver a letter to a total stranger!

"Thank you so much," I gushed.

Seeing the joy he'd brought me, his serious demeanor melted into a satisfied smile. I ran to the kitchen to grab some sweets, then planted them in his hand before saying goodbye. As soon as he left, I ripped open the envelope in the privacy of my room. Sam said he'd been thinking of me and looked forward to reuniting at an all-volunteer conference in Cape Coast around Christmastime. *Christmastime? I can't wait that long.* Besides, I had languished too long waiting for school to begin—a month and a half, to be precise. With no sign of the students arriving anytime soon, I'd have to take my first journey south.

While I looked forward to seeing Sam, I also needed a dentist as much as I craved letters from family and friends whose mail no doubt had been piling up at Peace Corps headquarters in Accra. Most importantly, I had decided to ask the Peace Corps director for a site transfer to another school. If I was going to thrive and not simply survive the next two years, I had to get out of Jirapa.

First, I needed to travel south to the city of Wa to buy a bus ticket to Accra. Fortunately, Sister Sue had already introduced me to Meredith, a younger Peace Corps volunteer living in Wa, who could help me navigate the process. Like Sister, she had arrived in Ghana the year before our group of volunteers. Serving as our regional representative, Meredith had already made plans to go to Accra and attend a VAC conference (a meeting of the Volunteer Advisory Committee, which functions like a student government). We agreed to meet in Wa the next week and travel together to Accra.

OFF TO WA

The morning I left for Wa, Sister walked with me to the main road outside St. Francis where I waited for the Tata bus. Between sentences, we paused to listen for the familiar rumble coming from the north. Ten or fifteen minutes later, the Tata came barreling down the dirt road. I picked up my backpack and stood at attention, but something was wrong. The bus was moving too fast. *The damn thing didn't even stop!*

Watching my ride come and go, Sister deduced the Tata was too full for more passengers. In its wake, I spat out dirt from a cloud of dust, cursing my bad luck. If I couldn't make it to the STC (State Transportation Corporation) in time, I couldn't buy a bus ticket to go with Meredith to Accra the next day.

"Don't worry," Sister assured me, "there'll be another one in a half hour."

Sure enough, another bus came. This time, there was plenty of room. I waved goodbye to Sister and boarded the bus. After a rocky hour-and-a-half ride, the driver deposited us in the commercial sector of Wa. Eventually, I found a Ghanaian to show me the way to a restaurant where Meredith and I had agreed to meet. Relieved to see her sitting at a table, I apologized for being late and ordered a snack and a beer—not just any beer but a delightfully cold one for a change. Meanwhile, highlife music blared over a speaker making it hard to talk. Meredith could see I was growing anxious, so we paid the bill and left for the STC building.

"You're probably going to have to wait a long time and kiss a big man's ass before you get a ticket," she warned.

"Great," I replied.

"Oh yeah, and that road over there will take you to the clearing that leads to my house."

"Thanks, Meredith, I'll see you later."

Nervously, I climbed up a flight of stairs to what I suspected was the ticketing office. After announcing my purpose, a middle-aged man explained, "He," *whoever that was*, "just took lunch." Pointing to two plastic chairs in front of a vacant desk, he instructed me to sit down. An hour or so later, the big man returned, eventually calling on the customer before me. After she left, I waited and waited, obsessively monitoring the clock on the wall as its minute-hand inched toward closing time.

Finally, he summoned me to his desk. Riffling through papers, he seemed to enjoy ignoring me. I looked down at my lap, concealing an eye roll. Obviously, I'd have to sweet-talk him into selling me a ticket. Feigning interest in his job, I managed to capture his attention. Finally, he produced a ticket from his drawer, holding it hostage in one hand while asking me out for a drink. *God, this was humiliating.* Having learned from my previous faux pas at Picorner, I cooked up an excuse and graciously declined his offer. This time, it worked. Relieved, I put the ticket in my bag and headed for Meredith's.

* * * * *

One of the safety nets that comes with exploring the unknown is a silent understanding between Peace Corps volunteers who extend their hospitality to traveling PCVs, whether they know them or not. Not only was it refreshing to be around Meredith, a younger volunteer for a change, but she graciously opened her home, sharing a meal with me that night.

It was then that I first tried a local brew called *pito*, an alcoholic concoction I'd seen fermenting, with flies sipping its froth, at the market in Jirapa. Meredith handed me a calabash and poured a small amount of the amber, bubbly liquid from a large jug. It had a weird, sour taste, like fermented apples and bacon. I guess, in the absence of beer, pito was the only alternative. By ten o'clock, we put out the lanterns and hit the sack. Tomorrow was going to be a long one.

Hearing soft beeping in the distance, I opened my eyes and sat on the edge of Meredith's sofa. It was two o'clock in the morning, which meant we had a half an hour to wash up and head out the door. Trekking across a rural clearing in the dark, a familiar ghost punched me out of nowhere. I stopped and clenched my stomach, doubling over in pain.

"Damn, I've got some intestinal parasite again."

A few minutes later, another one hit.

"Not much longer," Meredith assured me.

After covering nearly two miles, the first streetlight appeared, illuminating the way to the transport yard. As soon as we arrived, I launched into a sprint searching for a bathroom. Navigating a transport yard full of people and buses skewed in every direction was no easy feat, especially because the bathroom was at the opposite end of the yard, unmarked and basically two tiny shacks. Fortunately, I had packed toilet paper, heeding the Peace Corps motto: "Never leave home without it."

With time to spare, we found a chop stand and ordered coffee and fried egg sandwiches, then joined a long queue at the STC bus headed for Accra. It was well past our five o'clock departure time when the driver finally opened the door. Suddenly, the orderly queue erupted into a mad scramble. It was pure mayhem. People pushed and shouted, using elbows to beat the next guy to a seat.

"What the hell? Everyone has tickets," I protested. "What's the rush about?"

"It's always like this," Meredith said, smirking. "Drivers overcrowd buses to make extra money with bribes."

MY BIG TRIP SOUTH

The trip to Accra was a long, grueling fourteen hours. Once again, I found myself on half a seat, this time pressed against the ample arms of a large Ghanaian woman. Not good for the claustrophobic. At least the hard part was over; I was finally on my way.

Throughout our journey, the driver stopped at numerous villages and towns, the liveliest of which was the city of Kumasi. Located in the Ashanti Region of south-central Ghana, it was by far the most developed city I'd seen since leaving Accra months ago. I was told there was a lot of wealth in the area, stemming back to the days when Ghana was known as the Gold Coast. It quickly became evident, scanning the myriad markets, large commercial buildings, and women dripping in gold with fancy dresses and elaborate headdresses as they walked with their noses in the air.

Not long after leaving Kumasi, the bus picked up speed over paved roads, making for a smooth ride the rest of the way. It was dark and raining when we arrived in Accra. Exhausted, we hailed a taxi to the Peace Corps medical unit, hoping against odds to find a spare room to save money. Everything was closed. Out into the rain we returned, schlepping our backpacks through a wooded area to the Star Hotel. Once again, no luck. The hotel was booked.

Eventually, we found a room at the Continental Hotel. For a whopping 3,300 cedis a night (equivalent to $245 US today), we ended up staying at the second-most-expensive hotel in Accra. Oh well, at least the Peace Corps would partially reimburse Meredith with a travel per diem.

Early the next morning, I launched into fifth gear juggling a slew of logistics. First stop: Peace Corps headquarters. Buy stamps, post letters, pore over a stack of mail, and plunge into a box of goodies from Mom. Occasionally, I'd look up from my stash, eager to find a familiar face among the volunteers trickling in and out. At last, two of my favorite PCV guy friends showed up. We smiled and hugged each other, then talked about our sites. Next stop: The dentist, then back to headquarters.

By three o'clock I met with the assistant Peace Corps director. Having explained my reasons for wanting a site transfer, he seemed amenable if noncommittal, suggesting I first investigate a few schools on the western coast of Ghana. Luckily, I would soon be traveling there since it was on the way to Sam's site in Bogoso.

The next morning, I helped prepare programs for the VAC conference that Meredith and I attended that afternoon. Listening to PCV reps discuss their regional challenges and success stories gave me a healthy perspective; it also afforded me an opportunity to weigh in on how the Peace Corps might improve its bureaucracy like the long gaps in mail delivery. After the conference, Meredith and I were ready for some R&R at the American Club, an air-conditioned oasis where US diplomats and volunteers congregated to enjoy American food and drinks and relax in the lounge or outside by the pool. It was a much-needed respite from our lives in the Upper West.

On day three, I said goodbye to Meredith and caught a taxi to a transport yard where I struggled to find someone who could show me the bus leaving for Cape Coast. Everyone seemed unknowledgeable or unwilling to help. As it turned out, the buses were either booked or delayed. After a five-hour wait, I was finally on my way to Cape Coast.

The drive was delightful, with peekaboo views of the ocean sparkling between hills covered in tropical flora. I even spotted a few old forts high up on the hillsides. Unbeknownst to me at the time, these were the launching points where European traders enslaved Ghanaians, ripping them from their homeland starting in the 1500s. But that's another story.

Old fort in the background near Cape Coast

In three and a half hours, I arrived at Pat and Dave's house, an older Peace Corps couple who worked as teachers in Cape Coast. Luckily, another PCV whom I was especially fond of happened to be visiting them. Wholesome and kind with a Scandinavian look, Sarah seemed like a kindred spirit from the moment we met in Denver on our way to Alamosa. While the four of us swapped stories about our sites, I explained my situation in Jirapa, asking Pat and Dave to put in a word for me at their school. Hopefully, they needed a typing or English instructor. While Pat made dinner, Sarah and I walked to a nearby beach.

Passing palm trees glistening in the late sun, I took off my flip-flops and headed for the ocean. My feet reveled in the warmth of the sand, my nose and skin taking in the cool, briny scent off the Gulf of Guinea. Standing in the surf, I stared out at the waves, thinking about the vast differences between this tropical paradise and the hot, barren landscape that was my home in Jirapa.

"Hey," Sarah said, "I heard Sam might be staying at Busua Beach, a resort near my site. Do you want to go check it out?"

"Hell yeah, let's do it!"

The next morning, Sarah and I hired a Peugeot taxi to her site in Sekondi-Takoradi. After showing me her house, I asked her to reach out to her contacts, inquiring about a job at her school. Like Pat and Dave, she agreed to sync up with me in December. By early afternoon we headed back to the transport yard looking for a way to get to Busua Beach. With the help of two Ghanaian women, we found a lorry that could take us there. A highly unusual sight, these women wore cornrows, which I had been told was a sign of prostitution. Even stranger were the tattoos on their hands. I wondered if this, too, was a sign of prostitution or simply a tribal marking.

Unlike their standoffish city counterparts, these women, who spoke not a speck of English, graciously helped us, communicating solely through body language. Using arms and facial gestures, it was soon evident they were traveling in the same direction. Fortunately, we only had to wait a short time before the women waved us over to a lorry leaving for Dixcove, a small fishing village near Busua Beach. Along the lush coastline an old gray fort appeared on top of a bluff. As I'd later learn, Fort Metal Cross was built by the English in the late 1600s.

Moments later, one of the women tapped me on the shoulder and pointed toward the window before alerting the driver to stop. Sarah and I jumped out the back and waited for our next instructions. Pointing toward a rocky path through a lush hillside, one of them smiled and said, "Busua." We waved goodbye to our new friends, thanking them in Twi, "*Medaase paa.*"

It was a short trek to Busua which, thankfully, was nothing like a modern beach resort. Modest in scope, the resort offered thatched-roof bungalows and an open-air restaurant across from a postcard view of a little island framed by palm-covered hills.

"This place is really popular with Europeans and expats," Sarah said. "In fact, a lot of the volunteers are expected to come here over Christmas."

"No doubt, I will, too. It's like our very own *Gilligan's Island*. Hey, why don't we go see if Sam is around?"

After checking in with the manager, we found out Sam had already checked out. Fortunately, the rates were dirt cheap at 440 cedis a night. Since it was getting late in the day, we booked a bungalow and walked over to the restaurant where I ordered fish and rice for dinner. The next morning, Sarah and I returned to Takoradi before I caught a bus to Bogoso.

"Thanks, Sarah. I'll see you in December."

TRIP TO BOGOSO

The bus ride took only three hours, but it was horrendous every bit of the way. At first, everyone stood patiently in line, but as soon as the driver opened the door, a scrum broke out. People were now pushing and shoving each other to squeeze through the door. Quickly the seats filled beyond their carrying capacity as passengers spilled into the aisle jockeying for inches of foot space. Holding back from the melee, I waited for a spot at the front of the bus. By the time I boarded, there was barely enough space to stand on two legs. Instead, I made like a heron, standing on one leg with the other suspended over a putrid barrel of fish.

Within the first half hour, two large women on either side of me started arguing in Twi. One hissed, "*Saa?*" to which the other growled back, "*SAA!*" Back and forth they went as each exchange grew angrier. It was the equivalent of an American pissing contest where one threatens, "Oh yeah?" and the other shoots back, "Yeah!" For a moment, I imagined spears loosed in my direction, but a brawl was more likely. Fortunately, their aggression ended after exhausting rounds of threats.

Meanwhile, the bus jostled back and forth over bumpy dirt roads. With one free hand, I gripped a pole above my head, struggling to maintain my balance. Eventually, my arm grew tired, but switching arms meant contorting my body in a game of Twister. Throughout the journey, our driver stopped at endless potholes and road barriers where police or self-appointed militia—I wasn't sure which—ordered us to get off the bus so they could inspect our belongings. As a passenger explained it, they were checking for signs of smuggling or illegal profiteering since mines were in the area. Each time they inspected our bags, I wriggled my way up to a window, making sure my backpack didn't walk off.

Relieved to finally arrive in Bogoso, my next challenge required finding someone who could point me to the "white man's house," wording a PCV had advised me to use. Surveying the landscape, my eyes welcomed lush hills undulating in the distance with palm trees and pagoda-like houses perched on stilts. In a matter of minutes, I found a young man at a shop who happened to be a student at Sam's school.

Hills of Bogoso

"Yes, I can take you to Master Sam's," he said.

Master Sam's? How strange to hear him address Sam in the vernacular of slavery. As he guided me up a series of steep hills, the air hung heavily. Having grown acclimated to the heat and humidity, I was only vaguely aware of the wet shirt clinging to my body. Besides, my focus was elsewhere. I reveled in my bravery for having traveled alone through a new region of Ghana. But I was also worried. *Would Sam resent me for arriving unannounced?* A devilish grin crept up my face, anticipating his shocked reaction. Standing at the foot of his porch, the student called out for him twice.

"Master Sam, there is someone here to see you."

Finally, Sam opened the door. Looking down at us, he first greeted the student, then stared at me with vacant eyes. Puzzled, I looked up at him for several seconds until that old smile returned to his face. Only this time it was tenuous. Something was clearly off. Despite our history, Sam seemed ill at ease, as if he hadn't interacted with people in a long time.

"Come in," he said in stilted English.

By then, we had all learned to slow down our speech, avoiding contractions and enunciating like Brits when speaking to Ghanaians. But after entering his house, he continued talking in that stilted way.

"*Sam, it's me!*" I kept reminding him. "I'm American, you can talk normally now."

While giving me a tour of the house, I was shocked by his sparse accommodations. I couldn't stop myself from blurting out, "You have no kitchen?"

"No, but that's okay. I can use the bathroom faucet and a bucket for washing dishes."

Wow, he's worse off than I am.

Sam then showed me the bathroom leading to his bedroom, consisting of nothing but a cot by a window.

"Oh my god, Sam, how do you sleep on that thing?"

He shrugged, admitting it was no fun.

That evening, we cooked a meal together while sharing stories about our sites and the challenges we'd been through. It was then that I realized Sam hadn't seen a white person, except for a passing volunteer, since the Peace Corps first deposited him in Bogoso, which would explain the earlier awkward reception. By lantern light, we talked for hours at a small kitchen table, rekindling an old connection. Finally, his walls came down. In each other we found a safe haven, a place to refresh and renew ourselves before returning to the foreignness of our lives.

Acknowledging we were both tired, Sam picked up the lantern and reached for my hand as he'd always done, leading me to his room. That night, under a misty moon, we fell asleep in each other's arms listening to Simon and Garfunkel's "Bridge Over Troubled Water." The next day, Sam gave me a tour of his village before I left the following morning.

Exploring Bogoso

Back in Accra, I returned to the dentist and got my crown, then hung out at the American Club, stuffing my face with every conceivable food I had missed: hamburger, fries, pudding, lasagna, salad, ice cream, you name it. It felt like I gained five pounds in a day. The following morning, I hailed a taxi to the transport yard where I met up with a Ghanaian boy whom I'd hired to stand in line for my bus at four in the morning. By five-thirty, I took his place in line, dreading the journey back to Wa. It would be long and hard, hampered by an overstuffed backpack that I'd have to carry two miles to Meredith's house, assuming I could find it in the dark. The next morning, I'd have to catch another bus before returning to Jirapa.

SCHOOL BEGINS

On Saturday, November 15, I returned to a wholly transformed St. Francis. Girls were milling about singing and laughing, filling an old silent void with joyful activity. During my time away, the students had spruced up the field and readied the classrooms for school to begin that Monday. After greeting Sister, I walked down to the administrative office, eager to receive my marching orders. Good news: Not only would I be teaching ten typing classes a week to Form 5 students, but ten English classes a week to Form 3 students. Things were looking up, indeed.

Later, I played show-and-tell with Sister, pulling out mail and commodities I'd bought in Accra. Recounting stories of my travels, we drank beer while savoring some mini Babybel Gouda cheese, a rare treat in the Upper West since cheese was practically nonexistent.

"Hey, Sister, I have an idea. Now that I have cans of pumpkin and peas, plus a bottle of wine, spices, and marzipan for the Brits, let's invite the local volunteers to a Thanksgiving dinner."

"Sure," she replied. "I'll spread the word to some of the PCVs in the north."

Until then, it was back to the usual diet of sardines, rice, tomatoes, and onions.

* * * * *

"A, S, D, F, J, K, L, semicolon."

That was my mantra every day in typing class. Over and over, I recited the position of the typewriter keys to a handful of students who would then return to their seats, allowing for the next rotation of students since I wasn't provided enough typewriters for the class. Who knew teaching could be physically exhausting? After coming home drained from my morning classes, I started eating oatmeal first thing, which energized me through lunchtime.

English, on the other hand, was more fun. I enjoyed the challenge of quickly coming up to speed on British English. The word "learned" was now *learnt*, and "aluminum" now *aluminium*. Then there were incidents when the joke was on me. One day, a student spelled "dormitory" *dormitree*. Puzzled, I looked at her and shook my head. "No, that is incorrect," I said. "But, Madam, that is how we say it." Of course! She was merely spelling the word phonetically, much like "cemetery" is pronounced *cemetree*.

ALIVE

It was dark and quiet inside and out. At last, the girls were asleep in their dorms. Sitting at my vanity, a lantern glowed warmly to my right, its light bouncing off the mirror in front of me. After a long, hot day, my reflection was still kind. The temperature had only dropped a few degrees, but my skin was blissfully devoid of sweat after a cool wash-down. Combing my wet hair, I watched droplets of water trickle down my neck and shoulders.

I relished these moments of solitude when silence cleansed the mind as water to skin. I may have been exhausted, but one thing was for sure. I was alive.

I was alive because I didn't rush to dry my hair with a noisy blow-dryer. I was alive because I didn't need a man for approval. I was alive because my eyes and ears were clear and free of TV and radio. I was alive because I had learned to live with hunger in my belly. I was alive because I could laugh about the bat that just flew within inches of my face while brushing my teeth. A solitary vessel, I had become my own source of contentment.

THIRD-WORLD WORKAROUNDS

By the end of my first month of teaching, I learned to expect dysfunction. Most of my English students seemed infuriatingly slow until I realized their comprehension level lagged far behind the overly ambitious syllabus I'd been handed. Once their curiosity about my foreignness faded, they seemed oddly defiant.

Observing Ghanaian teachers yelling at them—some of the male teachers seemed to relish punishing the girls with yardsticks after making them bend over a desk—I deduced they'd been desensitized by punishment. If anything, they needed massive doses of positive reinforcement. To earn their respect, I practiced more patience, reassuring them without going overboard. As a British teacher observed, we Americans were far less formal than our British and Ghanaian counterparts. *Note to self: Tread carefully.*

As for typing, my Form 3 students and a new group of Form 4 students were only given two classes a week, not nearly enough practice time. Besides, the younger ones were too immature to treat typing as anything but a game. Considering the central role of music in Ghanaian culture, I concluded that for these young girls, clicking the keys was the equivalent of playing an instrument. Once again, my instruction to lightly tap the keys instead of smashing them seemed like an exercise in futility.

Sister Sue, on the other hand, capitalized on their love of music. One day, while walking past her classroom, I heard the students singing "Frère Jacques." *What? Science students singing?* I stopped to eavesdrop. As it turned out, they weren't singing "*dormez-vous, dormez-vous.*" They were singing "isotope, isotope." It was brilliant! She had plugged scientific terms into the lyrics so her students could at least memorize them by rote.

Students weren't the only challenge. The lack of organization at St. Francis, compounded by teachers who didn't show up for work or made their students late for my class, constituted ongoing headaches, not to mention the tedious staff meetings which often got personal. In response, I made like a wet dishrag, following the advice of my father who'd confronted similar obstacles on business trips in Nigeria.

By late December, Sister and I were running ragged. One day, she attempted to play hooky, something she never did. Within fifteen minutes, her students showed up at our door announcing they had come to "collect her." Sister played dumb, trailing the students to class while I stayed behind having a good chuckle.

Other times, I loved teaching, especially figuring out creative strategies to stoke my students' interest. One day, I had my girls on their toes raising their hands and asking questions. To capture their attention at the start of class, I offered toffees as a reward to the first student who could answer my question correctly. Holding out three toffees, I wrote on the chalkboard: "Toffees are _____ a cedi." As soon as a student gave the correct answer, "Toffees are three a cedi," the class erupted with excitement as they cheered on their classmate. *Ah-ha! Now I've got their attention.*

It didn't take much. In fact, the less I talked, the more effective I was. Every time a student was disruptive, I turned my back to the class and without a word drew a tick on the chalkboard, effectively silencing them. Not long after that, the girls were offering to erase the chalkboard and carry my books after class.

THE POWER OF MUSIC

A month before Christmas break, I recorded an audiotape as a gift for my family, sent with photos and a cover letter via a traveler going to Accra. The tape consisted of one-way conversations, a song I wrote and sang on the guitar, and a special performance by a Ghanaian boy.

Theo, my favorite among the campus boys who frequently visited us, approached me one afternoon while I waited on the side of the road for the Tata bus. Next to him stood a painfully thin friend in raggedy clothes, the whites of his eyes yellow and listless. Recognizing the signs of jaundice, I knew this boy was in trouble. Sister Sue, who volunteered at the hospital, recently told me Ghanaians were "dropping like flies" from hepatitis. Evidently, Harmattan winds were the culprit, spreading viruses from Burkina Faso down through the village.

Theo introduced me to his friend who seemed unwilling or unable a smile. "Play your instrument," Theo urged. Clamped in one of his hands was an empty soup can. "My friend made this himself," he said proudly. "Listen." Slowly, the boy plucked three strings tightly threaded to the open end of the can. In minutes, he transformed from listless to animated, playing staccato notes rapid-fire. It was like watching music feed life back into him through an intravenous tube. When he finished, I had tears in my eyes.

"Well done!" I said, clapping. The boy smiled timidly. Since he only spoke Dagari, I asked Theo to translate for me.

"Please tell him I want to record his song on a machine for my family. It would make them very happy."

A few days later, the two showed up at my door, eager to see a machine that could capture sound. After recording the song, I played it back watching their faces turn from curious to awestruck. Back and forth they grinned at each other, talking animatedly in Dagari. I had made their day as they had mine. While the machine no doubt left an indelible impression on them, it was the image of Theo's friend revived by music that stayed with me all of these years.

PUTTING ASIDE MY WESTERN LENS

One of my first lessons in seeing a diametrically different culture from a non-Western perspective came while sharing beers with two older Ghanaian women. One was Muslim and the other Christian. Both were friends. Despite my presence as an outsider, they launched into a lively debate, allowing me to join in on their candid conversation. It was the kind of day when customary niceties like "How are you?" and "I am fine" were pushed aside for real dialogue, the kind I'd craved since coming to Ghana. After all, candor was uncommon, at least in my presence as a foreigner.

Sitting in a field at a little wooden table, the two women compared whose lot in life was better or worse, weighing the merits of married life from both of their perspectives. Not since the days of sitting in front of the TV glued to *Nightline* had I been so engrossed in a conversation involving Islam. Until then, Western media had done its best acculturating the masses to view Muslims in a derogatory light, especially with regard to the treatment of women.

On the other hand, I knew that no group of people could be categorized with a broad-brush stroke. There were always reasons and always exceptions. It was Ted Koppel who first stoked my curiosity with his probing questions after the MS *Achille Lauro* had been hijacked by the Palestine Liberation Front. Once again, I was all ears.

Unsurprisingly, the Muslim woman complained of having to share her husband with numerous wives, with each playing a specific role such as the "baby-maker" or the "cook." Then the Christian chimed in, complaining about her husband's infidelity. Neither had the perfect marriage, but they both agreed on one thing: the benefits of companionship.

Unlike the Christian, her Muslim friend enjoyed a special camaraderie with her "sister wives," who provided companionship that the Christian woman lacked with her husband. Not only that, but there were other benefits. The Muslim woman confided that through her relationships with her sister wives, she could influence them to achieve a mutually desired result from their husband. If their strategy failed at home, they could always exert control over him in public, where his reputation was at stake. *Ingenious!* I thought, grinning to myself.

In the end, I learned that Muslim women weren't so powerless after all.

WORST TRIP EVER

Just when you think you've seen the worst, the Universe—in all its infinite humor—ratchets it up a notch. What was supposed to take a day and half to travel from Wa to an all-volunteer conference in Cape Coast turned into a three-day marathon, eclipsing my first journey to Jirapa, otherwise known as the Road to Purgatory.

From the outset, we were waylaid in Wa. Expecting to leave for Accra the morning after I arrived in Wa, we discovered our bus had been demolished in a crash due to Harmattan winds blinding the driver in a cloud of dirt. Two days later, at the obscene hour of one o'clock in the morning, Meredith, Brad, and I woke up and walked to the transport yard where we waited for a six o'clock bus to Accra. Once again, no bus. When the driver finally arrived, he was too tired to push on. Instead, we opted for a bus taking us far out of the way to Tamale.

Not having hit our quota of setbacks, the driver stopped in countless villages for every conceivable reason, from handing rope to a farmer to—well, you name it. Finally, about three-quarters of the way, we got a flat tire. Instead of waiting for a miracle, we hopped off the bus and hitched a ride in the back of a Mack truck. A few hours later, the driver dropped us in Tamale where we ran into some Peace Corps volunteers.

"Sorry, you're shit out of luck," one of them said. "There are no buses or planes leaving for another two days," exactly when we needed to be in Cape Coast.

Soon I realized there were eight of us stranded in Tamale, which was oddly comforting. If we were going to be late for the conference, at least there was power in numbers. After exploring our options, one of the volunteers lined up a deal with a lorry driver. *God help us because that means riding on a flatbed over rugged terrain.* For a whopping 1,150 cedis a person, the driver agreed to drive us to Kumasi at four o'clock the next morning.

In the pit of night, eleven of us, including two German volunteers and a Rastafarian from Burkina Faso, piled into the back of the lorry and slid down two opposing wooden benches beneath a tarp roof. On either side, our shoulders were exposed to the cold night air. Bundling up as best we could, we laughed off a palpable sense of dread. Shortly after departing, our luggage tumbled off the roof.

"*STOP!*" we yelled, banging on the side of the lorry.

Our bags disappeared beyond the red glow of the taillights. Finally, the driver slowed down and turned around, using his headlights to help us find our things. Fortunately, I found my backpack nearby in a ravine while the others collected their bags from the road. This time, I made damn sure he secured our things properly.

For the grand finale, we had three punctures and two near-accidents on the way to Kumasi. Never mind swallowing copious dirt and bruising our tailbones. Instead of eight hours, our journey stretched into eleven torturous hours. Over and over, we bounced up and down, our tailbones crashing against the wooden benches every time we hit a pothole or a bump in the road. Eventually, a German woman snapped, weeping uncontrollably. Somehow, I managed to morph into a stone, occasionally reaching for the cross and Saint Christopher medallion around my neck. *God, don't let me die. Not here, of all places.*

Finally came some comic relief when a militiaman pulled us over at a road barrier. Holding a fat Bob Marley joint, he opened the back door and looked around, asking if anyone wanted a toke. Of course, the Rasta obliged him, which put me on edge. *What if it was a setup?* Instead, the militiaman smiled and waved us on, bidding us safe travels.

By the time we arrived in Kumasi, I was ready to stay the night, but the majority wanted to push on. The only problem was, there were neither buses nor planes leaving for a few hours. Instead, we asked a Holy Roller for help. "God loves you and we love you, too. I will find you a ride to Accra," she said. Ten minutes later, she found us a *trotro*, an open-air, wooden bus with Jesus slogans painted on the sides. Once everyone had paid the driver and sat down, she stood at the front telling us to bow our heads in prayer before asking for a dash.

After circuitously crossing Ghana in a backward "S," we arrived late at night in Accra and checked into a hotel. Standing in front of a mirror, I was shocked by my reflection. My hair was a tangled bird's nest, my face, the color of dirt from forehead to chin. Staring back at me was a mammy face with white creased circles around my eyes. *What a cruel stereotype, as if slavery wasn't enough.* From *Gone with the Wind* to vaudevillian and minstrel shows, whites had been exploiting Africans for decades, most recently on the labels of Aunt Jemima products.

ELMINA'S PORTALS

After the Cape Coast conference, Robin and I decided to take a tour of Elmina Castle twenty minutes west along the coast. Perched on a bluff overlooking the ocean, Elmina was a whitewashed fort built by the Portuguese in the late 1400s.

Ghana, known as the Gold Coast at the time, attracted the Portuguese with gold and other rare commodities. Initially intended to protect their trade interests, Elmina later became a slave castle in the 1500s. By the 1600s, it was overtaken by the Dutch, followed by the British in the 1800s. For nearly 400 years, Ghanaians and other Africans were wrenched from their homeland, subjugated to unimaginable horrors across the transAtlantic slave route to Europe and the Americas.

While the tour guide spoke, I stepped up on a rock and peered through the portal of an old wooden door. Once my eyes adjusted to the dark, a cavernous dungeon appeared. In the distance, a filmy light poured through another portal. From my vantage point, traders once stood appraising Africans like human merchandise made to stand naked and cold in overcrowded conditions. The dank air filled my lungs, overwhelming me with nausea. I stepped down from the rock with tears in my eyes. The tour guide kept talking, but I couldn't hear what he was saying.

Later, he guided us up a staircase leading to the Dutch governor's quarters. Beyond a window overlooking a courtyard, the governor would stand on his balcony ogling female slaves. From there, he'd choose a woman to have escorted through a trap door to his chambers. If the slave became pregnant, she was allowed to keep the baby and give it the governor's last name. Finally, the guide pointed to a rampart overlooking the ocean.

"This is where many slaves jumped to their death before ever boarding a ship."

Gazing down at the surf crashing against rocks, I wondered if I could have summoned that kind of courage.

* * * * *

Flash forward to 1997, and I was back in DC at a movie theater watching a gut-wrenching story about an African-led mutiny on the Spanish slave ship *Amistad*. Wary the movie would hit a nerve, I didn't expect a torrent of tears. Wiping my eyes self-consciously, I glanced at other movie-goers who were clearly not as moved. After it was over, I walked out of the theater on legs as limp as linguini. It had been ten years since I toured Elmina Castle, yet it took until that day to realize how deeply I'd been marked by its portals.

WHIPLASH: RETURN TO JIRAPA

The contrast between the south and north of Ghana can give you whiplash. For a month, I glided in fourth gear along the coast, cheered by a faster pace and variety of life. The ease and conveniences of the south cast in sharp relief the deprivations of the north. From the cool breezes of Cape Coast and Busua Beach to the luxuries of the American club and embassy homes, I'd grown soft and spoiled over Christmas break.

During my last days in Accra, a strange melancholy hung over me. Recognizing the distant look in other volunteers' faces, I sensed we were all silently doing battle. While ready to return to a life of normalcy, I dreaded the isolation of Jirapa. Despite having requested a site transfer, the Peace Corps director insisted I stick it out until the end of the school year.

Returning to Jirapa required abruptly downshifting from fourth to first gear. Disoriented and depressed, I holed up in my room, reading, writing, and dwelling too often in introspection. The few times I tried to get away for the weekend, the Tata bus whizzed past me, overflowing with passengers. Watching it disappear in a cloud of dirt, I muttered at least once, "God, I hate this place." At least I now had a bicycle to get to the market.

Eventually it became clear my only choice was to sink or swim. I chose the latter, immersing myself in work. When school began, my workload increased from nineteen to twenty-five classes a week, the perfect cure for breaking out of a funk. Organically, I noticed a shift in focus from myself to my students. Whereas last term I worried about keeping up with the syllabus, this term I slowed down, making damn sure the students understood each lesson before moving on to the next. To hell with the school's timetable. At last, they were catching on. Finally, I could see a boost in their morale as well as our rapport.

In addition to teaching, I started tutoring a twenty-eight-year-old woman so she could learn how to type. Eager to increase her meager income from selling pito at the market, Sidonia came to St. Francis twice a week for lessons after class. More mature and motivated than my students, she picked up typing at a healthy pace. But I, too, was motivated. Seeing so many women dependent on men for security and status, my goal was to have Sidonia typing thirty words a minute by the end of the school term.

At last, I had a renewed sense of purpose.

THE UNVEILING

Life unfolded on its own terms in its own time. Cause and effect often eluded me in this strange new world I was coming to know. *Who are they? What's happening? Where is he going? Why is she sad? How did this happen?* Like a child extrapolating meaning from the unknown, these were the types of questions I found myself asking. More a spectator than a participant, I learned much about life, waiting on the side of the road for the Tata bus.

One day, I witnessed a woman wailing as she swung her arms back and forth, each time ending in a clap, on her way to town. A few minutes later, a bicyclist pedaled furiously behind her. Strapped to his back was a large bundle wrapped in a white sheet. *Well, that's a first. Men never carry babies on their back.* A second later, I realized the bundle was entirely covered. *What was inside the sheet?* I wondered. *Was the bicyclist related to the woman?*

Just then, a gust of wind pulled back the sheet, unveiling the head of a little boy. I strained my eyes in disbelief. His face was chalk white. Until then, I had never seen a dead Black person. *Did he die of meningitis?* According to Sister Sue, the virus was particularly bad that year, killing scores of children. Moments later, a procession of bicyclists followed the woman and the man with the little boy.

Like dominos dropping in slow motion, grief and death unfolded before me as I sat on a rock, confused, then shocked. Until then, I had never confronted the stark disparity between my privileged life and that of these Ghanaians. Even in death, we were afforded the dignity of a hearse.

Life, indeed, was unfair. But so, too, was death.

CHRISTMAS COMES IN FEBRUARY

My PCV friend Meredith recently returned from Accra bearing a care package from my parents. Shortly after arriving at her house, I thought, *Why not*? I ripped open the box and discovered an audiotape! I was so excited to hear my family's voices that I pleaded with her to let me play the entire tape on her boom box before going out to dinner as planned. It had been eight months since I last saw my family, and I hadn't received a speck of mail since last November. For her patience, Meredith was rewarded with peanut M&Ms and mint Milano cookies à la my mother's generosity.

Listening to the tape, I couldn't stop smiling. As soon as Mom and Dad started singing "Aba Daba Honeymoon," I squealed with delight as if listening to Lucy and Desi singing on *I Love Lucy*. With eyes welling, I beamed at Meredith, who was now smiling, too.

Then Mom's friend and my favorite neighbor, Joan Trudeau, joined in on a family conversation at the kitchen counter, catapulting me back to the comfort of home. Our counter may as well have been a fireplace. It was *the* congregation point for family and friends throughout my childhood. Between the familiar voices, mental flashbacks, and myriad goodies from home, it felt like Christmas had come in February.

To top it off, Meredith decided to pass her baton, appointing me the next regional representative of the Upper West. This meant I could attend the Peace Corps VAC conference in Accra next month.

TABOO AT THE MARKET

After teaching a few weeks at St. Francis during one of the hottest months, it was time for a change of scenery. Saturday morning,

I headed north to the village of Lawra where I decided to visit Brad. Much to my surprise, he was more animated and congenial than usual. He even introduced me to a Ghanaian friend, a soft-spoken young man named James. That afternoon, the three of us attended a traditional festival with drumming and dancing.

It was quite the spectacle, watching Muslim chiefs dressed in robes and caps beneath large umbrellas held by men ushering them onto the field. I was tempted to take pictures but thought better of it, recalling stories of PCVs who were suspected of spying for the CIA. Fortunately, Brad took a photo, which he later gave me (shown below). At the end of the festival, we went for a few beers at a local bar, where James and I hit it off.

Traditional festival in Lawra

The following weekend, James met me at the Jirapa market. I relished having someone to translate my many questions. After perusing the aisles, we sat down at a chop bar and ordered beers and fried bean cakes, the next best thing to Fulani cheese and *kelewele* (fried plantains rolled in ginger and cayenne), fast food I had missed since leaving in Tamale.

Everything was going swimmingly until I got an upset stomach. Since there were no bathrooms at the market, James guided me to a nearby compound where he asked a woman if I could use hers. It wasn't easy asking him for help since it was considered taboo to discuss anything related to the bathroom with the opposite sex. Hell, you weren't even supposed to greet people on your way to or from the bathroom. Fortunately, James had been exposed to Western culture since his father used to work at the Canadian embassy, so he seemed to understand.

The next thing I knew, I found myself standing in a concrete stall with a small hole in the floor. Flummoxed, I wondered why and how I was expected to crap into a hole. I suspected an error in communication, but my bowels couldn't wait. There was simply no time to ask for a toilet. After covering my poop with a tissue, I left the bathroom fearing I had committed yet another faux pas. Reluctant to confide in James—he was, after all, not only male but a new acquaintance—we returned to the chop bar to finish our beer.

Moments later, people were arguing on the perimeter of the market from which we had just returned. While I didn't understand Dagari, I knew the sound of a disgruntled woman. Suddenly, my heart started hammering. *Oh, God, if only I could crawl under a rock.* Then someone called James over to the quarrel. Trailing behind with my tail tucked low, I soon discovered the woman had actually accused James of bringing me there to insult her.

"What?" I ask incredulously.

"Yes, they think I brought you to their compound to insult them."

"How can they blame you? *You're* not responsible for my actions, and I didn't know I wasn't supposed to use that room until it was too late!"

Back to the market we went, painfully aware of what others were thinking. I didn't dare look up. *How could I ever show my face again?* After apologizing to James between fits of anger, I learned the hard way that there are two ways of asking for a bathroom: Either you say, "I need to urinate," which means peeing in a stall with a hole in the floor, or "I need the toilet," which means doing number two. I had no idea that "bathroom" didn't exist in their lexicon.

If only the Peace Corps had advised us how to navigate one of the most basic functions of life. But there was still much to learn. Indeed, land mines of taboos I'd inevitably step on.

INROADS AND HARD ROADS

March was insanely hot, the kind of hot that feels like a furnace blasting in your face. Even at nighttime, I'd lie awake covered in sweat. Toward the end of the dry season, the sun baked the roads rock hard, sending clouds of dirt into the air every time a vehicle passed by. At the time, rumors of horrific crashes circulated throughout the village. Even our school bus crashed into an articulator truck, injuring nine students and a teacher. Paranoid about traveling, I swallowed my fears and headed south to the VAC conference with a sack of letters from volunteers in my region.

Serving as our regional representative for the first time, I was relieved to make a few inroads. In the nicest way possible, I gave them holy hell after discovering several of my packages had been held up at Peace Corps headquarters since the previous year (three were postmarked October and November, and the fourth January). Skip, the veteran PCV who once admonished me for rejecting the advances of a chief of police, agreed to start delivering mail to the Upper West.

Another sense of accomplishment came from several PCVs who said they were shocked to discover I was still "hanging in there" since I was a city girl stuck at one of the lousiest sites in Ghana. Vindicated, I told them my secret to survival was traveling, at every opportunity. For example, with four days to kill after the VAC conference, I visited Robin up in Akropong, a tropical village in the Eastern Region of South Ghana. Since leaving Tamale six months ago, I had sorely missed my soulmate in crime.

While visiting Robin, we "took" lunch at an open-air restaurant (they say "take" instead of "have" a meal) when a curious group of Ghanaians stopped outside, sticking their heads through the bars above a wall surrounding the restaurant. With zero inhibition, they watched us obronis having lunch.

"See that?" Robin said, turning her eyes to the spectators. "I feel like an animal in a zoo. I'm so tired of people staring at me all the time."

I wanted to laugh, but Robin was serious. It's quite the conundrum, wanting to fit in but standing out as a foreigner. By then, we had both tasted what it must be like for minorities in the United States. But on some level, Robin opened my eyes to a reality I hadn't yet experienced. That is, until I headed north to Jirapa.

While the trip home was less physically taxing, it was emotionally eviscerating. Before taking off, I asked the bus driver if he had put my backpack below the bus along with the other bags. He ignored me, not once but twice. Even worse, none of the Ghanaian passengers were willing to help me grab his attention. Instead, they stared at me, muttering anti-American sentiments.

Livid, I crumpled into a puddle of tears. Weeping like a pathetic outcast, it was clear no one cared. For a long time, I stewed in a toxic medley of anger and resentment. The crazy thing was, the Peace Corps had told us that fifty percent of our purpose for being there was to serve as mini-ambassadors, spreading peace, goodwill, and cross-cultural understanding. Yet, times like these made it hard to muster an ounce of goodwill.

On the flipside, after returning to Jirapa, I discovered a silver lining about the north: Where I lived, Ghanaians, whom their southern counterparts derisively called "bush people," were far friendlier and certainly not as hostile as Ghanaians in the south.

SCORPION DANCE

Sister Sue had warned me of scorpions.

"Always check your slippers before putting them on," she said.

Since it was usually warm, I opted for flip-flops. The few times I wore slippers, I pointed a flashlight inside before slipping them on. Fortunately, many months had passed without a single sighting.

Then one day while walking home from class, something unusual unfolded before me. Ten yards ahead was a teenage girl—not a student but a worker—balancing a large basin of water on her head. Walking toward the home science building, she suddenly stopped within a few yards of a class in session. Frozen, she tilted her head ever so slightly, causing the basin to start wobbling. Back and forth it swung precariously, but something else was commanding her attention. With one free hand, she lifted her dress and carefully looked down.

Was she having her period?

Just then, she yelled something in Dagari. The girl must have called out for help because moments later, a teacher appeared in the doorway of the classroom. After they spoke, the students came pouring through the door eager to see what was happening. For some reason, the teacher spoke sternly this time, as if admonishing the girl.

Seconds later, she dropped the great weight from her head and shook convulsively while yanking at her dress. Then she darted toward the teacher, setting off a chain reaction among the girls who were now shrieking in that ear-splitting way of excitable teens. Instead of helping her, they turned around and ran back into the classroom.

What the hell? Why are they running from this poor girl?

As the teacher later explained, it wasn't her period but a scorpion crawling up her dress. Still troubled, I wondered whether the girl would've been treated more compassionately if she had been a student instead of a worker.

HIGH ON FREEDOM

During Easter break, I met an affable, easy-on-the-eyes agriculture volunteer named Mac. Several PCVs from my group and his were hanging out at the American Club in Accra when he invited us to an embassy home he'd been house-sitting for a diplomat. *Relaxing in the privacy of an air-conditioned home with every amenity you could ask for?* I didn't hesitate.

The diplomat's home oozed with opulence relative to our standard of living. I was practically giddy taking in the luxuries of a life I'd left behind in the States. After checking out his cushy pad, we made dinner and gathered around the TV to watch videos. Later, Mac and his friend, also named Mac, (whom I'll call Steel moving forward) asked if I wanted to go with them to Robin's house in Akropong. Delighted, I agreed to go the next morning.

Despite breaking Peace Corps' rule against using motorcycles for unofficial business, I had a blast riding on the back of Mac's bike through the Eastern Region. Not only were my arms wrapped around a hunk from the Midwest (by then, Sam and I had broken up), but it was my first experience on a motorcycle, which we called "motos." I loved the adrenaline of speed and a heightened connection to my environment. No longer did I need the protection of a windowpane separating me from my reality. Awakened by my own spontaneity, I tasted a kind of freedom I had never known.

After visiting Robin and her friend Jake, we agreed to meet at a beach in Apam later that week. Then Mac, Steel, and I headed north to Steel's site in Begero, a small village past the town of Koforidua. It was a real campsite—rural accommodations in a forested area, much like a ranger's station. That night, we walked to an outdoor bar and had beers and good conversation when out of nowhere Paul Simon and Ladysmith Black Mombazo started singing "Diamonds on the Soles of Her Shoes" over a nearby speaker. For a few moments, we sat quietly smirking at each other, surprised to hear a song we had last heard on the other side of the Atlantic. Talk about out-of-body experiences!

Later, we returned to Steel's house and sat on his porch overlooking a misty forest. Soft piano notes from a George Winston tape floated from Steel's boom box into the milky moonlight. Hypnotized, we sat quietly staring into the night. I must've been under a spell because later my feet guided me to Mac's room where I made the first move. A stocky guy with wire-frame glasses, dirty blond hair, and a mustache, Mac's brawn and brain had attracted me since day one. Trusting our chemistry, I was relieved my overture was well received.

The next morning, Mac and I were still waking up when Steel burst into the room blurting out, "Good morning, kids, it's breakfast time!" Bemused by his lack of decorum, we dressed and ate before heading out to see one of their favorite waterfalls. After parking the motos, we bushwhacked our way through a hilly jungle, with Steel in the lead swinging a machete. This was the Africa I had come to expect many years ago.

Climbing down steep terrain, I lost my footing and fell hard between two boulders camouflaged in brush. Stunned, I stood up on shaky legs and leaned against a boulder to steady myself. I looked down and inspected the damage to my left shin. *Shit, I got a hole in my favorite jeans.* Worse yet, I was staring at my shin bone where a layer of skin had been ripped back. Considering the macho nature of my companions, I couldn't exactly sit there and cry. After all, they were agriculture volunteers—code for "not wimpy," unlike the reputation they had given us education volunteers. I took a deep breath, rolled up my pant leg, and wrapped a bandana around the wound.

"I'm fine. Let's keep going."

Eventually, a beautiful waterfall appeared in the distance, cascading about forty feet into a water hole. Mac and Steel were now scaling a wall of slick boulders leading to a cave-like landing behind the rushing water. Battling my nerves, I made like a crab, clamping onto every crevice I could find. After reaching the landing, I stood behind the curtain of water crashing downward, its cold spray exhilerating my hot, sweaty skin. The sheer force of the water pulsed through my body like an electric current.

The next thing I knew, Mac and Steel had stripped down to their birthday suits and jumped in. Embarrassed, I looked away, then climbed back down to the water hole where I waded in my T-shirt and underwear. Pretty stupid, considering the risk of contracting giardia through an open wound.

The next day, we took off for Accra, then Apam the following morning. Once again, the freedom of traveling in the open air was insanely liberating. From the wind in my face to the ever-changing landscape, all of my senses came alive. Never having to worry about the next meal was equally as freeing. Whenever we got hungry, we pulled over at a roadside kiosk where bananas, pineapples, oranges, and peanuts were abundant. Simply put, living off the land allowed us to live in the moment.

Somehow (since there were no cell phones at the time), we managed to meet up with Robin, Jake, and some other PCVs at the beach in Apam late afternoon. After soaking up the sun and surf, I retreated to the cool shade of a palm tree. Moments later, a rainstorm caught us by surprise. Eager to find shelter, we hopped on our motos and rode into town where a pack of scrawny dogs chased after us, trying to nip at our legs. I wondered if our white ankles looked like chicken to them. Soon, we heard Highlife music coming from a bar that was buzzing with Ghanaians.

After downing a glass of water, we ordered a pitcher of beer. With liquid courage down the hatch, I got up the nerve to order bush rat for dinner. Served as a kebab, the meat was surprisingly tender. Thankfully, it was coated in ginger and cayenne, masking what otherwise would've been a gamey flavor. Reenergized, we joined the locals and danced for hours. Drenched in sweat and sorely in need of a shower, Mac offered to take me to a nearby fort doubling as a rest house.

Built by the Dutch in the late 1600s, Fort Patience was every bit as decrepit as one would expect, with bare-bone accommodations. In what seemed like a dark dungeon, I scooped up water from an old well to wash and shave—yes, shave my legs in the pitch dark while holding a torch between my teeth. I laughed at myself, hell-bent on having smooth legs for Mac.

To cap off a fabulous trip, we rejoined the others on the beach that night and sat around a bonfire before skinny-dipping in the ocean. The water glistened like black onyx under a full moon. Once everyone splintered off, Mac and I rolled around in the surf, giggling at the image of us looking like Burt Lancaster and Deborah Kerr in the 1953 film *From Here to Eternity*.

Sated, we returned to the fort and slept on a stone balcony overlooking the ocean. With only a travel cloth separating my body from the hard floor, it was hardly comfortable. But that night was pure magic. I wouldn't have traded the full moon and the lull of waves for an ounce of comfort. Besides, tomorrow promised a beautiful sunrise.

NO FOOD, NO SCHOOL

After Easter break, I returned to Jirapa only to discover my flat was in shambles. Dust, cobwebs, bat and bird turds were everywhere. We had no food, no water, and no kerosene. Nor was Sister Sue around. Even though I had bumped into her in Wa on my way back from Accra, she opted not to forewarn me. Instead, I had to learn from a campus worker that she was staying at the convent in town. Clearly, this was my penance for having committed the crime of traveling.

Off to the market I went, pedaling fast and furious, exorcising my anger. Besides, the market would be closing soon. After scouring the aisles, my heart sank. Most of the tables were empty, save for scant vegetables and fruit, most of which were spoiled. I had never seen things so bare, even at the end of a typical market day. All I managed to scrounge were some onions, a few half-spoiled tomatoes, and little else to prepare stew. Then again, we had no kerosene, so I had to resort to junk food from a care package.

The next day, I caught the Tata back to Wa to forage for food. The market in Wa was considerably larger than Jirapa's, but the supply of food was scarce there, too. Not even cans of tuna, my go-to protein, were available. To top it off, when I returned to St. Francis, I found out that school had been delayed, putting me in a foul mood.

Why did I bother returning to Jirapa in the first place? I dropped my bags in the kitchen and curled up on the couch, wallowing in my misery. Not only was I hot and hungry but suffering from giardia thanks to my own stupidity. Consequently, I started taking Flagyl, an antibiotic for parasites that play hockey with your intestines. The symptoms of giardia weren't nearly as bad as the side effects of Flagyl, which was why most volunteers avoided taking it.

FAMINE SEASON

Due to the long, hot dry season, food had dwindled well before Easter break. Back then, there were days I couldn't even find eggs, tomatoes, and other basic necessities at the market. Yams became our saving grace, which Sister and I ate on a nightly basis. To break the monotony, we alternated dipping slices of boiled yam in tubs of McDonald's barbeque sauce one night and honey mustard the other, thanks to Mom.

Then yams became scarce, too.

From April through June, barring my last trip south, I learned to live with hunger. To alleviate the gnawing in my stomach, I pressed three middle fingers into my belly and moved them in circles. For some reason, this seemed to dissipate my hunger pangs, probably because the pressure released pockets of air.

While I tasted real hunger for the first time in my life, knowing it was temporary came as no small consolation. If things got bad enough, I could always travel, which in turn deepened my sympathy for people who had no other choice than to go hungry.

SISTER SUE AND THE MIDNIGHT RAINS

Only Sister Sue and the midnight rains could bring out the kind of guilt in me that was exclusively the right of my mother and grandmother. All three shared an industrious streak that could drive a person mad. We're talking faithfully sweeping barely visible cobwebs in hard-to-reach-corners of the ceiling, okay?

Either I followed suit or faced retribution, usually in the form of Sister's silent treatment.

Although Harmattan had finally ended, the rains ushered in another chore. Even though we had access to borehole water, Sister insisted on collecting rain, usually in the middle of night. As soon as the sky cracked open, she dutifully donned her slippers and headed for the kitchen, clanking pots, basins, and buckets. After gathering her arsenal of receptacles, she'd tromp downstairs and line them up in the pouring rain.

Occasionally, I'd play opossum and drift back to sleep after hearing her go on a rampage. Other times, it was futile. Between the clanking in the kitchen, the loud claps of thunder, and the torrential rain lashing at our corrugated roof, there was no going back to sleep. What's worse, Mother Nature had a way of unleashing her fury around three o'clock in the morning. The noise was so deafening, we had to yell at each other just to hear ourselves. This, of course, was a convenient way of disguising our anger.

Compatibility, I learned, was the hardest chore of all.

CARVING A PATH WITH MY HEAD

May was a rough month. First, I informed our headmistress of my decision to transfer to another school after the final term. That didn't go so well. Since she'd recently returned from Accra, having met with my assistant Peace Corps director (referred to as "APCD"), I wanted to smooth over any potential misunderstandings. Nope, she wanted me to stick it out another year and give my Form 3s another chance, which was out of the question.

Second, my students' English papers were so riddled with errors that I wanted to pull my hair out. Unfortunately, both students and teachers spoke pidgin English, which didn't help matters. For example, instead of saying, "I went for a short time,"

Ghanaians would say, "I went small." Or instead of saying, "I have a pen," they'd say, "I'm having a pen." Trying to correct culturally ingrained ways of speaking was like carving a path with my head.

Last but not least, I was left in limbo waiting for my APCD to send a radio message on the status of my job transfer as promised. Consequently, I had to travel to Accra and firm things up. Fortunately, Sister Sue had already lined up a ride with a wealthy Lebanese man in Wa, who was taking her and a Franciscan nun to the airport in Accra. Thankfully, he allowed us to tag along.

MODERN MEETS PRIMITIVE

Sister Sue and I were sitting in the back seat of a Mitsubishi SUV, relishing a softer-than-usual air-conditioned ride. *So, this is what it feels like to be a "big man,"* I thought. Not only was it my first smooth trip in Ghana, but we'd made good progress, a far cry from public transportation with all of its stops for passengers, potholes, punctures, and police.

Whizzing in first-world comfort through a tropical area of the Brong-Ahafo Region, I stared absently out a tinted window. Suddenly, a bare-breasted woman appeared on the left. Wearing only a cloth around her waist, she climbed up a ravine to the edge of the road balancing a large basket of bananas on her head. Until that moment, I'd been disappointed not to see more primitive ways of life depicted on the pages of *National Geographic*. Witnessing this somehow felt redeeming.

How strange it was to be riding in luxury, observing such a hard way of life. Or maybe it wasn't hard to her; maybe it was me projecting my pampered American life onto hers. Then, as if in a wink from the Universe, a large commercial plane flew overhead as a bird crossed its path from below. *Flights, manmade and natural, juxtaposed.* I smiled to myself. *We are the plane; she is the bird. Who's to say which lot is better—that of those who live close to the earth or glide above it?*

The encounter brought back a memory of an extraordinary incident in Jirapa where, typically, nothing extraordinary ever happened. For over half a year, I had been living in the high desert, slowly acclimating to the foreignness of silence. Despite coming from a big city, where mowers, blowers, cars, and planes were the norm, I learned it wasn't difficult to "go native." Like country folk living in rural America, my senses had adapted to the quiet.

Which is why on an ordinary day something extraordinary happened. I was in the middle of a field when a distant rumble came from the sky. *It's still the dry season, so it can't be thunder*, I thought. Minutes later, the rumble turned into a loud roar. Overhead, a plane approached, the likes of which I'd never seen nor heard in Jirapa. Unconsciously holding my breath, I stared up at the steel behemoth, stunned as much by its power as the pounding in my heart.

In a matter of moments, my insular life had been punctured by a distant world. For the first time, I understood what it must be like for primitive people shielded from the intrusions of modern-day machinery.

LIGHT AT THE END OF PURGATORY

At last, my site transfer was approved! John, my APCD, informed me that I would be teaching at Datus Secondary School in the port city of Tema only thirty minutes from Accra. After meeting with John, I caught a taxi to Tema and met the school's proprietor and his wife, the headmistress, who gave me a tour of the campus. The proprietor, a cordial chief with a commanding presence, owned Datus Secondary School, among other enterprises.

Getting from Accra to Tema and back was easy breezy, literally. The coastal road was a pleasant drive with cool breezes coming off the shore where fishermen worked beside long wooden boats past rows of palm trees. As soon as I arrived in Tema, the first thing I noticed was a variety of commerce and transportation and diverse housing divided into community numbers. My school was located in Community 7, not far from the beach and significantly closer to my friends living in the south.

Fishermen on the coastal road to Tema

On my last day in Accra, John gave me my marching orders. I would need to be packed and ready to leave Jirapa the first week of July when he would pick me up and drive me to my new site in Tema. Finally, the long wait was over. At last, there was light at the end of purgatory.

NO REGRETS

With four weeks remaining in Jirapa, it was countdown time. Rather than a sprint, it felt like a slog persevering through midterms, preparing extra lesson plans to help my kids pass their final exams, and meeting with Sidonia twice a week to get her typing thirty words a minute. Once she achieved her goal, I helped her write a résumé and prepared a letter of recommendation so she could find office work instead of selling pito for a pittance.

In between the busyness of life, I found myself growing reflective, missing family and friends more than ever. It had been a long time since I'd last received word from home or seen a Peace Corps driver bearing mail. When I wasn't writing letters, watching them pile up on my desk, I journaled frequently. After all, isolation affords a lot of introspection.

Around this time, it occurred to me that it had been over a year since the Peace Corps had first extended their offer. Taking stock of my life since then, I realized how much I had overcome, adapting to the challenges of ever-changing environments, from Colorado to Accra and Tamale to Jirapa. I decided to check myself, mulling over thinly veiled judgments from Sister Sue, my father, and a British volunteer. All of them on various occasions had questioned the frequency of my travels.

The fact was my assignment felt more like a prison sentence than an opportunity to make a difference. Deafening silence, isolation, language barriers, extreme heat, chronic school delays, and a loss of privacy collectively threatened my sanity, compelling me to flee the Upper West at every opportunity. Whereas adjusting to Tamale taught me to put my physical health first, coping with Jirapa required prioritizing my mental health. If I was going to make it another year, I knew I needed stamina in body *and* mind.

Flipping the paradigm, if I hadn't traveled so much, I wouldn't have experienced much of what Ghana has to offer. Not its rainforests, jungles, waterfalls and beaches; not its castles, forts and history; nor its people and customs. All trumped anything money could have bought in the United States. Despite the hardships, I had no regrets. As my recruiter once told me, people who volunteered for purely altruistic reasons tended to burn out fast. And nothing, I mean nothing, was going to make me quit.

CHAPTER 5

Tema

LIMBO

After moving south on July 2, the first thing I did was visit Peace Corps headquarters and inquire about my mail. I hit the motherload! Not only were a slew of letters waiting for me but a care package containing an audiotape that my parents had recorded and a bunch of goodies and practical things like M&Ms, Slim Jims, and sponges.

While looking through my mail, several PCVs who'd just completed their two-year service came flowing into the office, eager to share their travel plans on their way back to the States. I grew envious hearing about their itineraries including Thailand, Denmark, and beyond. *Where would I go at the end of my service?* Suddenly, the world was my buffet. I was eager to taste everything it had to offer, but for the time being all I wanted was to move into my own place in Tema.

Soon, I found myself living in limbo, waiting for my house to be readied and for John to send for my belongings. (He never did pick me up in Jirapa.)

For nearly a month, I bounced between my friend Eleanor's flat, the Peace Corps medical unit, our director's house, and two hotels in Accra. Recognizing my restlessness, the Peace Corps director asked me to help with administrative work at a training program for new volunteers at Cape Coast University. I gladly obliged. It was a lovely area—lush foliage and a wide variety of birds by the ocean. I enjoyed getting to know the new volunteers and having a dorm room all to myself.

LOSING SAM

On the Fourth of July, USAID hosted a picnic in Accra for American diplomats and PCVs from around the country. While I'd never been a fan of Independence Day—after all, xenophobia is a close cousin of patriotism, blind to the sacrifice of Native Americans—it was a great opportunity to reunite with volunteers.

When Robin and another PCV (Christie) and I arrived, a large crowd had scattered across a lawn the size of a football field. Wafts of smoke streamed into the air from various directions where clusters of people had formed around grills. The familiar scent of hamburgers and hot dogs instantly evoked memories of home. After finding a sunny spot away from the action, we planted ourselves near some female volunteers from the previous group.

While Robin was talking, I overheard two women circulating the latest rumor. This time it was about Sam.

"Sent home? What do you mean? What happened to him?" I asked.

For some mysterious reason, the Peace Corps had medically evacuated Sam to the United States. I was crushed. Oblivious to my feelings, they continued feeding the gristmill.

"I heard he smoked some really bad pot," one of them said.

"I heard he was delirious because he hadn't been sleeping," said the other.

The more audacious their speculations grew, the more my shock turned to anger. *How dare they spread rumors about Sam, let alone within earshot!*

Since the early days of training in Colorado, Sam and Robin had become my core support system, a nucleus that sustained me throughout myriad challenges adjusting to life in Ghana. Sam and I may have stopped dating, but he still occupied a tender place in my heart. I grieved for him and ached for myself. Worst of all was not being able to say goodbye.

Just then, the national anthem played over loudspeakers, setting off something deep inside. Whatever it was kicked into automatic. My heart swelled on its own accord, catching me off guard. Music had a way of affecting me like this, which is why holding back my emotions was futile. Embarrassed, I looked down, concealing my tears. Much like my attachment to Sam, buried beneath was an invisible bond tying me to something greater than myself—a rootedness to place, the country I love.

Sometimes the body is wiser than the mind.

Fourth-of-July picnic with Robin and Christie

TEMA, AT LAST

By August 10, I finally moved to Tema. Having my own place again was like moving out of my childhood home for the first time. Bursting with joy, I couldn't wait to settle in and regain my privacy, something I'd sorely missed since leaving the States.

But I'd be lying if I didn't admit to freaking out at first. My kitchen had no sink, table, or shelves, nor my bedroom a dresser or closet. *Where the hell am I going to put my clothes and food?* But then I checked myself. *Denise, you've got your own damn place, not to mention a large bed and a living room with a couch, coffee table, and three chairs. Best of all, an electric refrigerator, unlike that freaking kerosene fridge in Jirapa! Had this happened a year ago, you wouldn't have handled it so well.*

Soon I began scouring the markets for household goods, from drinking glasses and a cutting board to pillows and an adapter for my fridge—no easy feat on a small stipend. Between jaunts to Accra, my neighbors started introducing themselves. Everyone was friendly and helpful, even the children who offered to teach me Twi, and two women at the school who invited me to a nightclub in Tema.

The only pressure I felt was to be out of the house by 7:30 a.m. or people started asking about me. Little did they know, I loved my alone time, but this was a very close community—literally and figuratively. Fishbowl syndrome would no doubt set in since I was a constant source of curiosity.

As for school, I was given only four archaic typewriters and told that I would be teaching only one English class five times a week. Then came news that school would be delayed until October unless more students start enrolling. *Breathe deep, Denise.* "Take time," as Ghanaians say.

STREET LESSON

I was shopping in a crowded market along Accra's bustling streets when a woman cried out, "TEEF!" from behind. Turning around, I scanned the crowd and spotted a woman who was clearly shaken. I noticed she had no purse while she pointed in the direction of the thief. The next thing I knew, a mob had formed, funneling through the crowd in the direction of the thief who by then had disappeared from view.

The image stayed with me until I returned to Community 7. I worried for the man and asked my neighbors what the mob might do to him.

"They will beat him, even to death," one said.

It was instant street justice. Or was it? To me, mob justice was no different than a pack of animals chasing down its prey. The thief had no chance to defend himself, let alone a day in court. Either he was lying somewhere beaten to a pulp and/or breathing his last breath.

Many years later, I recalled that police were scarcely around if at all; besides, there were no phone booths to call for help or report a crime. If people hadn't come to that woman's rescue, how could she have hoped to get her purse back? And how could they have been sure the thief wouldn't return to steal from them?

In the end, I learned not to judge a culture based on my Western lens but on its own terms, thanks to my former professor and dear friend, Elaine Hagopian.

GLORIA, MY GIFT

As it turned out, our assistant headmistress happened to be my neighbor. Within a few days of moving in, Gloria Koram crossed the hard dirt between our houses and introduced herself, then her husband and three sons, all belonging to the Fanti tribe of southern Ghana. Reserved at first, Gloria exuded a quiet strength, dispensing smiles only sparingly. Her discerning air let me know I could trust her. In fact, the first lesson she taught me was not to trust anyone too eager to be my friend.

"If they're eager, they want something from you," she warned.

In the beginning, Gloria kept a respectful distance but was always helpful and cordial. As our relationship warmed, she lowered her armor, laughing easily with me. Through a silent knowing, Gloria seemed to understand the nuances of my culture in the United States, no doubt because her husband traveled extensively for StarKist.

Compared to Jirapa, assimilating to Tema was a cakewalk. Life's hardships were fewer and less daunting, as were the novelties I once faced in Jirapa. Whenever I confronted challenges assimilating to Tema, Gloria was there to help smooth the way.

Gloria Koram and family

Take, for instance, the day my Peace Corps director and his wife came for a visit and drove me to the local fish market. Having recently tried octopus kebabs, I pushed aside my squeamishness and brought one home to cook. As soon as I returned to Community 7, I walked over to Gloria's asking how to prepare the octopus. Without hesitating, she offered to clean and scale it. All I had to do was tenderize and fry it with butter and lemon juice. Not bad.

Gloria also offered tips on how to prepare Ghanaian meals. But whenever I added a spice that diverged from tradition, I was doing it wrong. But that was fine. I simply waited until she left, then tweaked it with the spices I preferred. Eventually, I learned from her and other women in my community that you don't mess with tradition. I guess Ghanaian recipes are so old they're carved in stone!

MICE AND RATS SPELL TWILIGHT ZONE

During my first week in Tema, I'd lie awake at night, listening to the sound of scratching coming from the wall behind my dresser. Night after night this continued, but I never encountered the culprit.

Finally, evidence of nocturnal visitors appeared one morning. After waking up, I walked to my dresser, opened a drawer, and reached down for a shirt where I discovered mice poop strewn all over my clothes. Disgusted, I asked Gloria for advice. Following her suggestion, I bought some rope and hangers, then rigged up a clothesline between my louvered windows and bedroom door. That was the easy part. Then all my clothes had to be removed from the dresser and put on hangers within the first week of moving in.

Deducing the shower drain was their only plausible entry, I covered it with a rubber lid thinking *problem solved*, until one day I came home from Accra and found shredded food wrappers scattered across the kitchen floor. *What the hell?* Sure enough, the rubber lid had mysteriously moved inches from the drain. Obviously, the barricade was no match for rodents determined to break through my box of prized junk food from the States. After that, the Peace Corps helped me nail a metal screen to the drain and gave me a piece of wood to seal the gap below my front door.

HOW TO WASH YOUR DOG

Gloria laughed with me as I stumbled through the assimilation process, but the real laughs came when she discovered peculiarities about my culture. One day, after I'd given her a few magazines sent by my mother, she walked toward my house holding one of them as if she herself had caught a mouse. Visibly struggling to contain herself, she said, "Look," pointing to an article on how to wash your dog.

"How to wash your DOG?" She could not stop laughing.

Gloria didn't quite articulate it, but such indulgences clearly seemed ludicrous. For starters, it was uncommon for Ghanaians to have pets, which, generally speaking, were neither seen nor treated as sentient beings. Animals existed to serve human needs such as food and labor, and little else. Besides, water was a luxury in Ghana. The last thing they'd consider was wasting it on a dog, let alone looking up tips on how to clean a dog. Conveniences taken for granted in the United States, such as running water used for dishes and showers, were practically nonexistent in Ghana. Simply accessing water was no easy feat for many people.

Although I no longer needed to carry water from a borehole or a rain barrel, I now had to hold a bucket under the showerhead to collect water, then dump it in a pot, which I would then heat over the stove to wash dishes. With a bucket of dishes in soapy water and a pot of hot water, I'd sit on my front stoop and scrub the dishes before rinsing them off. Which is why preoccupations with washing one's dog now seemed ludicrous, even to me.

LOSING ROBIN

By October 6, I finally started teaching. What a relief it was to be fueled by purpose again. School started off on a positive note, but I still had no sink and, worse yet, no Robin. Due to health concerns, the Peace Corps sent her back to the States for medical tests.

One afternoon, anticipating her return, two PCVs and I took a bus to her site in Akropong where we toilet-papered her house after dark. (In hindsight, I shudder to think what the locals thought.) A week later, I learned that she wasn't coming back. The Peace Corps had administratively separated her. I was devastated.

Not only did I lose a close friend but my soulmate in crime. Only Robin shared my deviant streak and propensity for misadventure, perhaps because her mother and my father came from the same hardscrabble hood in Somerville, Massachusetts. *How can I finish out my last year without her?* Reeling, I returned to Tema and fell into a funk.

Deprived of the opportunity to finish out her service, I knew Robin was furious, but I was lost. With Sam gone, Robin was my last anchor without which I felt adrift. After all, best friends are like mirrors; they remind us who we are. In need of solace, I prepared to visit Mac the following weekend.

GHANAIAN HOSPITALITY

As soon as school let out Friday, I took a bus to the Volta Region in the southeast corner of Ghana. Leaving the city, my chest filled with pride. I had never been to the region, let alone Mac's site in the village of Lolobi. Like my trip to Bogoso, I would once again arrive unannounced. After eight hours of traveling in pouring rain, which would've taken half that time if our bus hadn't broken down, the driver pulled over in the village of HoHoe (pronounced "hohoy") five miles south of Lolobi.

It was eight o'clock at night when I found myself stranded in a transport yard illuminated only by a handful of headlights. Desperate, I pleaded with one driver after the next to take me to Lolobi. No one was budging. The roads were too bad. My heart dropped. *What the hell am I going to do?* Eventually, a lorry driver took pity on me.

"I know a Roman Catholic priest who can help you," he said. "Follow me."

After walking a short distance through the village, he introduced me to the Ghanaian priest who, indeed, offered to put me up for the night. I thanked the driver, attempting to dash him money, but he refused.

Expecting the priest to show me to my room, he first ordered supper for me, then brought two beers to the table and struck up friendly conversation. I couldn't believe my good fortune. Nowhere in the States would I ever have expected this hospitality from a stranger. Then again, I'd never found myself in such dire straits.

The next morning after breakfast, I thanked the priest who asked a young girl to show me to the taxi rank. The road to Lolobi was so muddy it took an hour to cover five miles, but seeing Mac's smile again made it all worthwhile. Fortunately, I had packed a can of oysters and a bottle of wine before leaving Tema since all he had was rice for dinner. The following morning, we laughed in bed, cocooned beneath his mosquito net.

"Good morning," he called out to his hog through the window.

Later, we brought coffee outside and sat on a bench watching a young Ghanaian boy climb a tall, slender pawpaw tree several yards away. Effortlessly, he scaled the tree, wrapping his long, skinny limbs around its trunk. Every now and then, he'd glance down at us to see if we were looking. Clearly, the boy was accustomed to plucking its fruit, but this time, his prize was another kind—the impressed look on our faces.

"I bet you can't do that," I said, goading Mac.

"Watch me," he replied.

As soon as the boy hopped off the tree, Mac started climbing it, albeit more slowly due to his stocky build. Two thirds of the way, he stopped and flashed me a satisfied grin, his arms flexing in the filtered light of the forest.

"Nice muscles," I said.

Buoyed by each other's company, we walked five miles back to Hohoe. After boarding the bus, I turned around for one last look. There was Mac, waving goodbye.

WHERE'S BLACK PAINT WHEN YOU NEED IT?

School was going "slow-slow" as Ghanaians say. My archaic typewriters had finally been fixed, although I still had only five while I'd been promised twenty-one. Similarly, I had to make do without English books and a classroom dedicated to typewriting. Instead, I winged it in English and shared a classroom with another teacher, which meant corralling the students every day to haul the typewriters to and from class. In short, Datus was ill-prepared at the start of the term. Not only that, but, as I'd soon discover, my students needed to unlearn poor studying habits.

What I needed was a weekend getaway, so I took off with Mac and a Canadian volunteer and hung out at a nearby beach. Later, we got in trouble for sleeping too close to the president's residence. We had no idea! The police detained us for a few hours, then released us without incident.

The following Monday, I prepared for class and taught nonstop until three-thirty. Back at my house, I was wolfing down lunch when two acquaintances came calling at my door. "Where have you been?" one of them asked. "We had planned to do things with you last weekend," the other said.

While I appreciated the sentiment, I felt torn by their expectations. On the one hand, I knew it was important to develop relationships with people in my community; on the other, I was reluctant to get too embroiled since jealousy over friendships with Americans tended to run high. In short, your business becomes theirs. I'd heard about the fallout from other PCVs who'd grown a little too close to the locals in their community. One of them, my friend Nadine, unfortunately ET'd. She was the third to go, bringing our group down from twenty-one to eighteen volunteers.

Over time, I realized the source of my tension *was* their attention—whether it was the unabashed stare of strangers or the curiosity of neighbors observing and commenting on everything from how I did my laundry to when I came and went. Fishbowl syndrome had finally set in, so much so that one morning I lay in bed fantasizing about pouring a bucket of black paint over my body. Yes, it had reached that point. Some days, when I wasn't teaching, I deliberately hid in the privacy of my home, reading for hours. It's a strange thing, wanting to assimilate knowing you can never blend in.

WHEN ONE DOOR CLOSES: THE LAMPTEYS

In the months following Robin's departure, I felt more alone than ever. To console myself I reached for platitudes. *Everything happens for a reason . . . when one door closes . . . blah, blah, blah.* Eventually, a door did open. No longer able to lean on my closest friend, I made a concerted effort to get to know the Ghanaians around me. After all, my wish had finally come true. I no longer had to live in isolation. Now I could easily communicate with literate people in my community. Soon, I befriended a Ghanaian family who took me under their wing.

It all started the day Rex Lamptey introduced himself at a local watering hole called Point 7. Graying at the temples with a broad smile and dark complexion, he came over to my table, asking if he could join me.

"Sure," I said.

"Where are you from?" he asked.

My answer must've tickled a bone because he just sat there grinning until moments later, he blurted out a familiar jingle:

"Citizens Bank of Maryland, conveniently yours."

"*What*? How do you know that?"

Here was this Ghanaian singing a tune I'd grown up with on the other side of the Atlantic, my bank's very own advertisement! Laughing, he explained that he had attended the University of Maryland before earning his law degree in Ghana.

"A barrister?" I asked.

"Yes, what you call a lawyer," he replied.

Gregarious by nature, it wasn't long before Rex invited me to meet his family, who lived several blocks from my house.

His wife, Alice, was a small woman with a sweet smile and a quiet demeanor. He then introduced me to his daughters Pat and Ruby and his sons Joe and Charles. All of them were polite, if perplexed by their father bringing home a stranger, let alone a young American woman. Later, I learned they belonged to the Ga tribe from the southeast coast of Ghana.

After meeting everyone, Ruby offered to show me the way back to my house, exuding the same confidence I'd seen in her father. While Ruby and Pat were younger by eight and six years respectively, it didn't matter. In time, I was delighted to have "sisters" to hang out with and a barrister who had my back. Besides a budding camaraderie with the Lampteys, I knew it was important to have locals looking out for me.

When I wasn't teaching, I'd hang out at their house or take the girls to a chop stand for goat kebabs and soda or beer. Other times, they'd visit me at my place. I cherished our conversations and the many opportunities to learn about their culture. One of my favorite memories was a day trip to Labadi Beach with Pat and Ruby. Later that afternoon, we befriended a Lebanese man who invited us to join him and his wife for a generous spread of delicious food. We jumped at opportunities for cross-cultural exchanges like these, but best of all was the simple pleasure of hanging out at the Lamptey house.

To this day, I still laugh at a memory captured in a Polaroid photo. One afternoon, while Mama Alice was pounding cassava and plantain on her back patio, she persuaded me to give it a try. Taking hold of a long, wooden staff, with my hands placed all wrong, I was afraid to use all of my strength, fearing I'd crush her hands as she slipped water over the white, starchy blob soon to become fufu. Meanwhile, Pat, Ruby, and a neighbor stood nearby having a grand old time laughing at the obroni. My arms started shaking right around the time my lower back began to ache. Although making fufu takes about an hour, I lasted only fifteen minutes. Then I handed the staff back to Mama Alice who called out for Joe's assistance.

Later that night, I joined the Lampteys for a Ghanaian feast of fufu and groundnut stew. Midway through the meal, Ruby whispered in my ear, divulging that her parents had slaughtered a goat earlier that day to make my favorite kebabs. I covered my mouth, feeling honored and humbled.

Mama Alice pounding fufu with Ruby and Pat looking on

Not only did I cherish my newfound sense of belonging, but the many social outlets the Lampteys provided. Rex, the girls, and I frequently hung out at Point 7 where I could always count on good conversation, whether silly or substantive. To spice things up, Rex often invited others to our table. Usually, they were foreign because, like me, he was fascinated by people of different cultures.

Out with the Lampteys at Point 7

Over time, the Lampteys adopted me, just as I had them.

CUBAN NIGHT

Of all the patrons Rex could've invited to our table at Point 7, this time he asked a scary-looking group of Cuban men to join us. All four were broad and burly with brooding demeanors. If I had seen them in an alley, I would've run in the opposite direction.

"Please, come join us," he said, gesturing over to our table.

Considering Rex's small stature and the fact that I was a young blonde, it was the first time I questioned his overtures to strangers. The Lamptey girls had already advised me to stay clear of Korean businessmen rumored for hiring prostitutes. After all, Tema was a port city, attracting international trade and all kinds of foreigners. But this? This was pushing my boundaries.

At first the Cubans hesitated, appearing to consult each other, but then they sat down at our table and thanked us for the invitation. I greeted them with a lukewarm smile, letting Rex take the lead at introductions. Next, he called for the waiter and ordered a round of beers, a Ghanaian custom I grew to love. Regardless of one's income, Ghanaians generally paid for their guest's food and drink, knowing the favor may or may not be returned one day. Splitting the bill was out of the question. Not only that, but Ghanaians usually poured their friend's or guest's drink before their own.

Once the Cubans were served their beers, a long, awkward silence followed. I wasn't sure who felt more uncomfortable, the Cubans or me. Despite Rex's solicitous nature, they seemed reluctant to speak.

"No hablo inglés," said one of them.

"Solo un poco," said another.

For the next hour, we fumbled our way through a clunky exchange of English, Spanish, and body language, with Rex and me laughing every time we inadvertently reverted to Twi. Eventually, the Cubans relaxed, as did I once the scariest guy broke a smile. Turns out, our guests were sailors who had recently docked in Tema.

By the end of our exchange, the Cubans were no longer menacing. They were merely men who missed their families after having been away at sea for months. This would explain, at least in part, their brooding countenance.

A week later, we ran into them again. This time, I was at Point 7 with an American friend and most of the Lampteys when Rex called the sailors over to our table. After a round of beers, he invited them to his house for dinner the next night. They readily accepted his offer, catching me by surprise. But Rex knew better. He wanted to provide them a sense of home and family, something they'd dearly missed.

Before the Cubans arrived, the Lampteys and I had prepared kebabs and bought beer for our guests. That evening, these once scary men showed up at the door carrying a large crate of food from their commissary—a generous gift of cheeses, fruit, and canned fish. My eyes practically popped when they pried open the lid. Secretly, I hoped the Lampteys would share the cheese, but more than anything I was touched by the generosity of these sailors. Coming from Cuba, they couldn't have had much money.

Handicapped by our language barrier, we resorted to food and music. After a while, we realized the easiest way to communicate would be through a game of charades. As the British were fond of saying, it was brilliant! Communicating through body language and a few key words helped us to connect while providing lots of laughter.

Toward the end of the evening, Rex presented the Cubans with a tray of glasses and a bottle of *akpeteshie*, a locally distilled spirit made from palm or sugar cane. Since akpeteshie was pure fire water, we warned our guests, explaining this was Ghana's version of tequila. It was so strong they were blown away by the first sip. Seeing these burly men grimace made me want to laugh but I knew better.

By then, I was blown away by a different kind of spirit—the spirit of camaraderie between people from vastly different cultures. Better than cheese, Rex gifted me this legacy.

SECOND CHANCES

Rex Lamptey

CRANKY ME

By December, I started losing my ability to laugh. School was so poorly run that I stopped caring whether anything got done. One day, like any other, I went to school expecting something would surely prevent me from holding class. Sure enough, a bunch of students were out on the field practicing for a soccer match during school hours. When I asked a teacher whether we were having classes, he said he didn't know but he'd send someone to tell me. No one ever came.

Day after day, adapting felt like dog paddling. Sometimes I got so exasperated I wanted to bash my head against the wall. Laziness, dysfunction, and a weak work ethic were endemic. Making matters worse was an authoritarian educational system that trained students, especially girls, to stay silent and memorize by rote instead of participating in class and comprehending the material. *Ramming speed! Keep up with the syllabus or else!*

What's the point? They're not learning anything if all they're doing is memorizing for a passing grade.

Meanwhile, due to a shortage of functional typewriters, I resorted to using only one to teach my students. Though hardly optimal, my classes were small and frequent enough that the students didn't have to wait too long for individual lessons. I started out each class by having the kids recite the keys illustrated on the chalkboard, reminding them where to place their fingers. One by one, I called the students to the front of the classroom where they each received hands-on practice. For the time being, it was the best I could do. Besides, Christmas vacation was only three weeks away. I couldn't wait.

FINDING GRATITUDE

My lousy attitude wasn't exactly parting the clouds. If I couldn't change my circumstances, I could always change my outlook. I started practicing gratitude, jotting down positive aspects about my life in Tema compared to DC: living in flip-flops 24/7 (no closed shoes, thank you very much); coming up with creative workarounds for the classroom; physically exerting myself, pushing boundaries instead of buttons; living in the fresh air versus artificially sealed environments—all were a boost to my health, both physically and mentally.

Conversations were less artificial, too. I became a better listener and an avid reader, thanks to well-read volunteers rubbing off on me. In my spare time, when I wasn't reading, I'd lie on the couch and look up at a world map I had pinned to the wall, memorizing the capitals of countries. I knew if I had a TV or a phone, I would've been distracted from doing things that enriched my mind. Bit by bit, or *nkrankakra,* as Ghanaians were fond of saying, I found contentment.

SECOND CHANCES

WITH A LITTLE HELP FROM MY APCD

Eventually, problems at school started clearing up. After writing a letter to my APCD, making my case for a dedicated classroom and more typewriters, he called the school proprietor and threatened not to replace me with a new volunteer next year. Miraculously, the proprietor called the headmistress, and all of the sudden I had a classroom filled with thirty tables and chairs.

My APCD then assured me he'd follow up with the proprietor to ensure I received more typewriters and a secured classroom. *How nice it will be, not having to chase after students to help me lug them to and from class every day.*

With my spirits lifted, I no longer felt the urge to leave Tema on the weekends. I didn't even crave long-distance travel as I used to in Jirapa. After three months in the south, my familiarity with the students and friendships with Ghanaians gave me a sense of belonging. Unfortunately, another door was about to close. My neighbor and friend Gloria Koram, would be leaving Datus in a month or so. *I will miss her dearly.*

MEKO BRA (I GO COME)

One of several things I learned to say in Twi was *meko bra*, or "I'll return soon," which literally meant "I go come." Lately, the students had been doing a lot of that. They kept leaving school to collect fees from their parents, since most weren't able to pay the lump sum up front. And because our school needed more students—in other words, money—they accepted new students at any point in the term. They went and came so frequently, I didn't even recognize my class some days.

For more fun, our proprietor kept hiring part-time teachers who were invariably late, causing disruptions and delays to the full-time teachers' classes. We had to cancel so many classes that we couldn't even give a proper final exam. Over and over, I found myself following my father's advice to make like a wet dishrag.

FOOD CHAIN

You'd have thought it was a national holiday, the way people were whooping and hollering in the streets. In actuality, it was more like the first rain after a long, hot dry season, only it wasn't water falling from the sky . . . it was locusts, thousands of them, descending on Tema.

I was at home having dinner when I first heard the commotion. Immediately, I put down my fork and walked to the main street where a communal frenzy had erupted. People of all ages were running around in the dark, laughing and calling out to each other, slip-sliding in their flip-flops over crushed locusts. One swarm was met by another. Everyone reached into the sky, grasping handfuls of locusts like children scrambling for candy falling from a piñata. Some of the women even collected them by cupping their dresses.

Thoroughly grossed out, I returned to my house and discarded what was left of dinner.

* * * * *

Another night, I encountered a different kind of swarm, this time in my bedroom. I was reading a book under my mosquito net when the sound of buzzing and tapping caught my attention. Looking upward, flying cockroaches flicked off the heat of a bare lightbulb while others ricocheted off my walls and mosquito net.

Buzz-buzz, tap-tap-tap. I lay there frozen in disgust. Weighing my options, either I could remain a captive or make a mad dash for the light switch. I mustered the courage to turn off the light, then scrambled back under the protection of my mosquito net.

This went on for several nights until one morning a visitor appeared. Staring down at me from my bedroom wall was a mossy green gecko. *Jesus, what next?* Just then, I remembered geckos are the good guys. Soon, he became a welcome guest.

"Good morning," I'd say. "Stay as long as you like."

Indeed, the gecko had taken up residence, enjoying free buffets until, finally, the flying cockroaches were no more.

* * * * *

Locusts and flying cockroaches aside, there was a different kind of prey in Ghana. Well, at least in some parts. Before my friend Nadine left Ghana, I had agreed to adopt her cat, Casey. This time, I would be more careful since my previous cat, Bear, had taught me a harsh lesson about life.

When I first came home with Bear, a young, fluffy black cat, Pat Lamptey warned me, "Take care no one chops him."

"What do you mean? People do *not* eat cats here," I insisted, calling her bluff.

"Yes, sometimes they do," she said, grinning.

After that, I kept a close eye on Bear. In just a week's time, he left a dead mouse on my living room floor.

"Gross! Why did you leave that *here*?" I demanded.

Another time, he came into the kitchen carrying a dead mouse.

"Good for you," I said, realizing that was his way of presenting me a gift.

Not only did the mice disappear but eventually Bear, too. Worried, I asked my neighbors and the Lampteys if they had seen him, but no one had. Unfortunately, that was the end of him. I never did find out if someone "chopped" him, but I figured if they were hungry enough to eat a cat, I couldn't blame them.

A TASTE OF LUXURY IN TOGO

After school let out for Christmas break, I attended our annual three-day conference in Cape Coast, then worked at Peace Corps headquarters, editing and typing our newsletter, *The Talking Drum*, plus several training programs for the administrative office. With work out of the way, Eleanor and another PCV and I hired a taxi to Lomé, the capital of Togo, across the eastern border of Ghana. None of us had plans before Christmas, so what better excuse for a little adventure?

The differences between Lomé and Accra were vast. The roads were wider and well paved without the traffic congestion, pollution, and litter characteristic of Accra's streets. Then again, it was Christmastime, which would explain why the roads were nearly empty. Along the coastal highway, tall, modern buildings sprang up from the nearly sea-level capital. Everything seemed cleaner and better maintained, including the bathrooms, which actually had toilet paper.

Another difference was that, unlike Ghana, Togo was a francophone country. Having gained independence from France in 1960, the Togolese spoke French and a little English in addition to their local dialects. Many people in Lomé belonged to the Ewe tribe, a handsome people with high cheekbones and almond-shaped eyes who lived on both sides of the border between Togo and Ghana. I noticed they seemed friendlier than the average city folks in Accra.

Our first stop was at a European hotel where we paid to use an Olympic-size pool for the afternoon. Compared to the fancy clientele draped around the pool, I felt as frumpy as a Peace Corps volunteer in Birkenstocks. But who cared? We were only there for a swim and lunch, after which I gasped at the bill. Later on, following Eleanor's suggestion, we hit a grocery store and made like Europeans, buying French baguettes, wine, cheese, and fruit to bring back to our hotel.

The highlight of the trip came later that evening. Back in our hotel room, I waited anxiously for a phone call from my parents. As soon as the telephone rang, I sprang up from the bed and picked up the receiver.

"Hello. Denise?"

My mother and father were both on the line. For the first time in seventeen months, I talked to my parents over a telephone. How wonderful it was to hear their voices. I rambled and rambled until I could hear the cash register ringing in my dad's head.

"Okay, this is costing you a fortune," I said. "Thank you so much for the call. I love you. Merry Christmas."

The following morning on Christmas Eve, we found a rooftop restaurant with black-and-white decor and linen tablecloths, reminding me of a French café. Our breakfast was yet another taste of luxury. The coffee, served in white, round ceramic cups, surpassed anything I'd tasted in Ghana (usually instant Nescafé). And, *oh my*, the warm, flaky croissants melted in my mouth. As if they weren't buttery enough, I couldn't resist the sweet French butter served on the side with jam. It was such a treat that I tucked a few of the foiled-covered pads into my purse. As volunteers on a meager stipend, we had learned to take advantage of freebees when and wherever we found them. From there, we hired a taxi back to Tema.

Unlike the ride to Lomé, our return to Tema was hot and tiring. It took three and a half hours stuffed in the back of a Peugeot taxi with five other passengers. Between getting through customs, running out of gas, stopping to put water in the radiator, and pulling over at police barriers, where we waited for them to inspect our bags, I couldn't wait to get back home.

"Akwaaba," said my neighbors, welcoming me home.

"*Medaase*," I replied.

THE GIFT OF BELONGING

On Christmas Day, I walked over to the Korams' house with a gift or two. In exchange, Gloria gave me a Kente scarf woven in orange, black, green, and maroon, a generous gesture considering the expense of chiefs' cloths.

"*Medaase paa,*" I said. "This will be a nice token to remember you by."

From the Korams, I headed over to the Lampteys, who had invited me to spend Christmas with them. Right away, I noticed there was no Christmas tree in their living room. I wasn't particularly surprised, but the absence of its magical presence left a void. Knowing the children had only received one gift each, I passed around their presents with great pleasure.

Instead of indulging in all the material trappings of Christmas, I enjoyed simply hanging out with the Lampteys, singing songs, and sharing stories. In the absence of a Christmas tree and my own family, I received the greatest gift of all—the sense of belonging.

POST-TRAVEL BLUES

Before the second term started on January 12, I caught the post-travel blues. Although I had looked forward to getting back into a routine, I found myself holing up inside my house. It didn't help that I had spent so much time with Americans over Christmas break. Just the idea of returning to my life with all of its daily dysfunctions cast a heavy blanket over me. Unlike returning to Jirapa after traveling, this time was different. It wasn't a crippling silence or isolation. *So, what was it?*

As usual, the new year had a way of making me wax reflective. Flipping through the pages of a wall calendar, I stared down the next six months of service as if looking up a steep mountain.

Although challenges were no longer daunting or novel, I found myself easily agitated at the slightest provocation. With an end in sight, all the things I had learned to suppress to fulfill my role as a mini-ambassador came bubbling up to the surface. At any given moment, anything—a reckless driver or a school delay—could cause my cork to blow. Weary of introspection, I buried my melancholy in a good, long book.

In a few weeks' time, I snapped out of it. It was good to be back at work again. Besides, the students and I were now on a familiar basis and Datus had finally provided a lab to keep the typewriters in. At last, no more chasing after boys to help me carry them to and from class. Even though I only had eight typewriters, my students were more serious in smaller groups. They learned faster from individual attention, and I didn't have nearly as many disciplinary problems. Better yet, my Form 2 students were finally catching on to their English lessons. At last, progress.

DISCO NIGHT

One Friday night, Ruby and Pat asked me to go out dancing with them. What a blast we had at the local club, boogying until closing time by which point our clothes were plastered to us from sweating. (They were amazed to see a white person could dance.) The real fun came when the DJ slowed things down, playing "Holding Back the Years" by Simply Red, a popular song back in the States at the time. After the first few notes, I was incredulous.

"That's my favorite song!" I yelled out to Pat and Ruby.

Beneath a mirrored disco ball, the three of us stood there beaming at each other with sweat glistening on our foreheads. Just then, I snapped a mental picture of us, a breathless triad of sisterhood emanating pure joy. Like a mantra, I kept singing the lyrics, "I'll keep holding on," absorbing the emotion behind the words. Words that girded my determination to get through the next six months. Words that at the same time echoed my gratitude for those brief shining moments.

Sweat evaporates, but song permeates the mind and body, leaving indelible memories. Thirty-six years later, "Holding Back the Years" still transports me back to those moments in time.

FAMILY DAY

Yesterday was family day at the Lamptey house. After lunch, I pulled out my guitar and sang a few American songs. Then Rex put on some Ghanaian highlife and South African tunes. Despite our best efforts to sing each other's music, it soon became clear our styles were wildly different. That's where singing diverges from dancing. The body adapts to foreign rhythms far more easily than the mind and throat can mimic them.

Later that evening, Mama Alice came out of the kitchen with bottles of beer, groundnuts, and kelewele. Strewn across the living room floor, we chatted about each other's cultures, exchanging stories from our past. Then I remembered to pull out some recent photos of my family, which pleased them. After dark, I returned home, feeling lucky to have such nice friends as neighbors. That night I fell asleep hoping to one day return their hospitality in the United States.

MISSING HOME

I was listening to the *Voice of America* on my shortwave radio when a reporter announced that the Redskins would be going to the Super Bowl. Instantly, my mind flashed back to Maryland. I would be missing one of the biggest football parties my parents and their friends were sure to throw. Suddenly, I found myself yearning for home and everything I associated with football season: the crisp autumn air and falling leaves, warm fires, and bowls of chili. Just then, I picked up a piece of paper and wrote home. A month later, I would learn about another headline in a letter from my mother: The federal government had banned smoking in all of its offices.

"You'll have to quit smoking," she chided me.

Instead, I focused on going back to college when I returned to the States. By then, I'd resolved to take it more seriously, so I wrote Dad a letter asking him to request my college transcript and look into admission requirements for schools with journalism programs.

I looked forward to returning to college, but also enjoying the simple pleasures of daily life in the States: watching TV, working out on a carpeted floor, shopping for groceries and cooking meals on the weekend, going on bike rides in DC, sitting on the porch reading the Sunday paper, and dressing up in high heels for a night out on the town. Then again, since leaving the US, many of my friends had gotten married and were now having babies. *How strange. I'll be on a completely different track when I return to school.*

IN SICKNESS AND IN HEALTH

One morning, I woke up feeling like my body had been used as a punching bag the night before. I ached all over, my head throbbed, and I had a temperature of 102. *Was I in a brawl?* Disoriented, I had to think about whether I had partied too hard the night before. *Nope, I stayed home.* Then why was I sweating profusely? My night shirt was soaked. Not good.

After dragging myself out of bed, I walked over to Gloria's, asking if my symptoms sounded like malaria. "Yes," she replied.

At first, I panicked but then remembered malaria was like the common cold to many Ghanaians. *Let's see if I can sweat it out.* By noon, I had no energy, and my clothes were soaked once again.

With a renewed sense of urgency, I walked over to the Lampteys, asking if one of the girls would go with me to the Peace Corps medical unit. Surprised by their puzzled look, I wondered if I was being alarmist. The fact was, I was so limp I could barely stand. Fortunately, Pat agreed to go with me, and we caught a taxi to Accra.

Over the next two days, my fever grew worse. With a stubborn temperature of 105, the nurses jumped into action, escorting me to the shower. Swallowing all sense of modesty, I stood there naked with one of the nurses holding my arm while the other poured ice water over me. Still, the aches continued. Then one of the nurses sent for a doctor, who gave me a painful shot of quinine in the ass. The needle must've been six inches long because I couldn't stop myself from letting out a loud moan. Then came several tests. Turns out, I had a severe urinary infection mimicking the symptoms of malaria. Weird. Evidently, a case of UTI had affected my kidneys, causing body aches and other symptoms.

After several days of air conditioning and American food, I was almost reluctant to return to Tema. As soon as I felt better, I called Datus Secondary School, letting them know what had happened. A few days later, the nurse put me on a three-month course of antibiotics and sent me home. All in all, I had been lucky the past year and a half, having escaped any major illnesses. Other PCVs hadn't been so lucky. Some even got malaria twice. In fact, just the other week, another PCV had been medically evacuated.

As soon as I arrived in Tema, I couldn't believe the outpouring of concern. Neighbors, kiosk women, even strangers asked how I was doing. Ever since Pat went with me to the medical unit, the

Lampteys had received numerous inquiries about my health and whereabouts. Perhaps that's why Rex wrote the following letter to the Peace Corps director expressing his concern:

> *Dear Sir,*
>
> *Denise Colbert is a volunteer who has been assigned to Datus School Tema and lives near my house. She is a regular visitor to the house and a good friend of my daughters and family.*
>
> *Last Thursday 18/Feb/88 she took ill with what was suspected as a fever and she was accompanied by my daughter Pat to the Peace Corps office. She was taken to hospital and was admitted. We do not know which hospital she was taken to, and she has not phoned the house or the office. We do not know what is going on and we are worried and sad.*
>
> *I have dispatched my daughters to try to locate where the hospital is (starting from your office) and to visit her. We have keys to her rooms in Tema and will bring in any personal effects she might need.*
>
> *Kindly help the girls to locate her. We miss her so.*
>
> *Yours faithfully,*
> *Rex Lamptey, Barrister at Law.*

Deeply touched to read his words on legal letterhead, I felt bad for being the cause of so much worry. I may have disliked the local gossip, but it sure paid off if you were in trouble. Ghanaians, strangers and all, looked out for each other in sickness and in health.

WHILE THE TEACHER'S AWAY

After convalescing for two weeks, I returned to work only to discover most of my classroom chairs were missing and only two out of seven typewriters worked. Did anyone substitute in my absence? Of course not. Instead, the students had played with the typewriters while the teacher was away. Not only that, but instead of showing up for class that morning, my students were out on the field practicing marching for Independence Day. Did anyone tell me they had been given permission? Of course not. Nothing was more frustrating than preparing for class only to make a U-turn home. This went on for a few days, but then again, it was nothing new.

At the start of the term, my students missed school because several were sent home to collect fees; before midterm break, my students missed school because they had to practice for a sports competition; after midterm, my students missed school because they had to practice marching. Such was my life as a teacher.

Once the repairman finally came to fix the typewriters, my last remaining thorn was a male teacher who habitually hogged up my periods. Inevitably, he'd make my students late for class or pull them out before the period ended. The aggravations were enough to make me want to quit. After voicing my frustrations to my APCD, he asked if I wanted to go home.

"Hell no," I replied. No way was I going to let anything prevent me from finishing out my service. Instead, I made like a wet dishrag, taking solace in the knowledge that other PCVs were equally fed up, if not burned out—that and the fact that many had already ET'd or been medevacked or separated. It was a feat simply having gotten that far. Thankfully, my Ghanaian friends kept me sane and laughing. Besides, spring break was just around the corner.

In April, the Peace Corps would be holding our Close-of-Service (COS) conference for those of us finishing out our two-year service. It would be a time to reflect on the past two years and prepare for reverse culture shock after returning to the States. Until then, I decided to save money for my last trip north.

THE THRILL IS GONE

By late March, it was so hot, not even the kiosk women were selling eggs because they spoiled too fast. Living under a corrugated roof made the heat all the more oppressive from noon until nighttime. Often, I felt sluggish, making it easy to procrastinate chores like sweeping and doing laundry. There were days I would've given anything just to plop a load of wash into a machine.

In fact, Ruby sometimes chided me for ignoring the mountain of dirty clothes accumulating in my bedroom. Sometimes, she'd ask to help me wash them, and a few times I gladly obliged. Once we got going with a bucket of water and bar of soap, I enjoyed her company as much as the physical activity. Both had a way of reviving my stamina.

One morning, the heat finally broke. I was lying in bed enjoying the cool air when the wind picked up, blowing sand through my windows. Dark, ominous clouds had gathered outside. Quickly I closed the shudders, threw on some clothes, and dashed out the door to buy some bread. Within minutes, the sky broke loose, sending a cold, hard rain down my body. Instead of running for cover like usual, I stopped and laughed, enjoying the thrill of the rush.

On April 1, school let out for spring break. The first thing I did was catch a taxi to Peace Corps headquarters and check for mail, hoping I might run into a few volunteers from my group.

Several familiar faces trickled into the office, but this time something was off. Instead of being excited to see each other, most were in a daze, lost in thought. Perhaps they were focused on leaving their communities or making travel plans on their return home to the States, but the energy had definitely shifted.

After talking with several PCVs, one thing was glaringly apparent: Nothing seemed to faze us anymore, not someone coming down with malaria or someone being medevacked to the States. Rarely did people complain anymore; if someone did, it was usually met with a sarcastic reply. In other words, the thrill was gone. With one leg in Ghana and the other in the future, we had already begun our departure.

AKOSOMBO: CLOSE OF SERVICE

Later in April, I met up with the education and agriculture PCVs in Akosombo of the Volta Region for our Close-of-Service conference. The Volta Hotel was one of the nicest accommodations I had been to in Ghana. Next to the lobby, tall, wraparound windows with sweeping views of the Volta River enticed customers into the restaurant. Nearly as airy were the meeting rooms—all in all, a great place for our final reunion.

After our last working session, Eleanor and I wandered outside where several PCVs were trying to form a human pyramid in a large pool. Seeing them struggle, I jumped in the pool and climbed up to the second tier. Standing on the shoulders of PCVs below us, we steadied ourselves, arms locked, and feet balanced. Then Brad, being the lightweight of the group, was appointed the third tier. Up he went, clutching shoulders and climbing over our backs. Halfway up, he fell off the pyramid, then scaled it again. This time, he mounted both tiers, standing victoriously on top. Now *that* was teamwork!

Without moving, I looked out of the corner of my eye, making sure Eleanor was taking photos as I had asked. There she was, doing me one final favor. Just then, the pyramid collapsed into the water, ending in a big splash.

On our final morning, we gathered outside for a group photo before saying goodbye. Standing in front of a large boulder, both education and agriculture volunteers stood side by side for the first and last time. *Would we ever see each other again in the States?* Indeed, we would, some of us remaining lifelong friends.

LAST TRIP NORTH

After the COS conference, I headed north with Pat Lamptey and a PCV friend from the second-year group. My goal was three-fold: pay respects to Afryea in Tamale; give Pat a chance to explore her country; and visit a few volunteers in places I had yet to explore. Three-quarters of the way to Kumasi, our bus driver pulled over for a brief break. By then, all of us were tired and irritable. Clearly, Tema had softened me. Nothing seemed worth traveling on half a seat over rough roads anymore. Four hours later, we arrived in Tamale.

Immediately, we set out to find Afryea, my live-in host during training. Not having seen her since moving to Jirapa, I had no idea whether I would find her. First, we walked through my old community where familiar faces greeted me along the way. After stopping to ask a former neighbor if she still lived there, I was crestfallen to discover she had moved.

"But I know where she is working," the neighbor continued. "You can find her at the district office in Tamale."

I thanked her profusely. "*Medaase paa, paa, paa!*"

Back to town we went. Somehow, we were able to find the district office where I inquired about Afryea.

"She is working here?" I asked an older woman.

"Yes, I will find her."

Smiling, I turned to my friends. "Oh my god, you guys, we found her!"

Several minutes later, Afryea appeared, looking dignified in office clothes. I smiled and stood up to shake her hand, but she seemed oddly distant. *Oh shit, did I do something to offend her? Maybe she's just hiding her surprise.* Thankfully, she agreed to meet us for lunch at the market. After we all sat down at a table, the fond expression I was used to seeing finally returned to her face. How wonderful to see her warm smile again. Afterward, Afryea invited us to dinner the following night.

When we arrived at her house, the table had been set. Afryea was much more at ease this time. Later that evening, she honored us with fufu and a delicious groundnut stew. By the end of the night, she took my hand and told me that my visit after so much time was a true sign of love and respect. For once, I was relieved to have done something right instead of committing a faux pas. Our brief time in Tamale provided the closure I needed while giving Pat and my PCV friend opportunities to mix with Americans.

From Tamale, we took a bus to Wenchi, a PCV town in the Brong Ahafo Region of Kumasi. The terrain was lush and less populated than Tamale, with houses constructed mostly of mud and thatched or tin roofs. It was the closest thing to what I'd consider a jungle, with the exception of the Volta Region. For the next few days, we visited Delia, an older PCV known as the "mom" of her group. Delia was a great host, living up to her reputation by feeding us well.

The next morning, she took us to a water hole to go swimming. By the time we arrived, I started feeling feverish with back pains. Swimming alleviated the sweats, but as soon as we settled down for a picnic, my symptoms kicked in full throttle. Back at Delia's, I took my temperature. It was 104. Fortunately,

I had remembered to pack some malaria pills, which eventually brought my fever down to ninety-nine. Who knows if I had malaria. My symptoms were similar to dysentery, dogging me the entire way back to Accra.

When we arrived in Accra, it was too late to check into the Peace Corps medical unit.

Fortunately, I ran into our new APCD at the American Club, who offered to put us up for the night. Having recently completed his service as a PCV in Burkina Faso, he related to us much better than most of the staff. How delightful it was, basking in a warm shower and a comfortable bed with air conditioning!

PLANNING AHEAD

After returning from spring break, my attention splintered in a multitude of directions. Organically, teaching took a back seat as I prepared to leave Ghana. There was much to do. I pulled out my list and started checking off tasks:

- Get performance review and recommendation letter from the school proprietor. Check.
- Get headmistress and Peace Corps director approval for your final day of school (June 24). Check.
- Next: Book flights to Cairo, Athens, and DC; sell guitar and radio; take COS physical exam at Peace Corps headquarters; prepare, hand out, and grade final exams; return books to administrative office and get clearance form; give away household items; pack and head to Accra.

Waves of excitement and melancholy played with my mood. I knew where my travels were taking me, but what lay on the road ahead? Where would it take me? I was excited to visit Cairo and Athens but equally eager to get home. Putting down my pen, I stared at the faces of family and friends pinned to my wall, photos that would soon be packed away. *How much will I have changed in their eyes and how much will they have changed in mine?*

SEND-OFF, LAMPTEY STYLE

On June 4, the Lampteys threw a big party, inviting relatives and neighbors to celebrate Ruby's graduation and the end of my two-year service. I brought popcorn, chips, and beef for kebabs; the Lampteys provided beer, soda, and other snacks. All night long, we sang and smiled, dancing to Western pop and Ghanaian music. Every time I attempted to speak Twi, the elders lit up, emoting their pleasure with big gestures and sounds, a Ghanaian trait I had come to love.

The highlight came moments after Rex played a traditional Ewe song. Suddenly, everyone stopped what they were doing, making a deep guttural sound like *woah*. The next thing I knew, Mama Alice and some older women got up from their chairs and joined the crowd on the dance floor. With a flourish, they rolled up their sleeves, placed their hands on their hips, and started ululating. As if on cue, they morphed into chickens, flapping their arms and thrusting their chests in and out. The girls and I laughed so hard we cried.

What a wonderful send-off!

COUNTING THE DAYS

As my departure date approached, I rejoiced in no longer having to flip a page in my calendar. Instead, I relished marking off each day. It was hard to believe I had only two weeks left before leaving Ghana. *Hallelujah, I made it!* The days may have grown anticlimactic, but I was high on the fact that I had nearly completed my service.

In the second-to-last week, I gave my students their final exams and spoke at their morning assembly. Leaving customary formalities behind, I enjoyed taking off my teacher's hat and speaking to them on a personal level. Afterward, the students came to my house off and on throughout the day, bringing letters and gifts and requesting photos. Everyone's kindness—that of my students, fellow teachers, neighbors, and the Lampteys—made me realize the impression I had made. Despite all the frustrations, I was rewarded with gratitude.

Then came more send-offs. First, Datus Secondary School threw me a lovely party with a large turnout and a generous array of food, drinks, and gifts. Then the Lampteys invited me to dinner at their house on June 25.

It was my last night in Tema, and like two years before in DC, my last supper with dear friends. But this time was different. Back in DC, I was confident I would see Carol and Jack again, but I knew I'd never see the Lampteys in their home again. That night, for the first time, I left their house with a heavy heart. My only consolation was knowing I'd see them once more at the airport in Accra.

BEERFUL GOODBYES

After moving out of my house in Tema, I stayed in Accra at the Star Hotel with my PCV friend Delia while wrapping up last-minute business. She was a great support throughout an anxious time, offering to ship back to the States a beautiful hand-carved wooden chest—a generous gift a student had surprised me with, one that I would cherish for years to come.

Then, finally, July 3 came. It was my last day in Ghana, and the Lampteys had hired a car to see me off at the airport a few hours before my flight. After a final round of one too many beers, I hugged my Ghanaian family long and hard, unable to stop the river of tears gushing from my eyes. Finally, I pulled away, saying "*Yebehyia bio.*" Until the next time.

* * * * *

It's been over half a lifetime since I left Ghana, but thanks to one of the more positive aspects of social media, I've been able to reconnect with Ruby and Pat after many years. I am now happy to report that in 2024, we shall indeed meet again, only this time in Europe where they currently live.

AFTERWORD

My story of second chances resulted in a personal transformation—indelible changes that have stayed with me all these years. As our Peace Corps trainers told us to expect, we would indeed experience a transformation upon completing our two-year commitment, one that would enable us to carry out Peace Corps' third goal: to promote a "better understanding of other peoples on the part of Americans." Put another way, returned volunteers facilitate peace by fostering understanding and empathy for people from vastly different cultures.

Transformation, however, can only happen after meeting the Peace Corps' first two goals: (1) helping people of interested countries in meeting their need for trained men and women, and (2) helping to promote a better understanding of Americans on the part of the peoples served. Only then can volunteers transform by developing a "third entity."

Let me explain.

When we first arrive in our host country, we are purely American. When we assimilate to our host country, we adopt its customs and culture. When we return to the States, we are no longer wholly American or, in my case, Ghanaian, but an amalgam of both—a third entity. Which is why reassimilating to the States is often challenging for returned volunteers. Simply put, our perspective broadens, so we see things differently. And in seeing things differently, we're often at odds with the status quo and eager to find fellow misfits.

An example of the challenges we face upon returning to the States is best illustrated by a story my mother recalls about the first time she took me to a grocery store after I returned from Ghana. Since the Peace Corps had already prepared my parents (and the other volunteers' parents) in a letter advising them of the reverse culture shock often experienced by returned volunteers, my mother was on guard that day.

As she tells it, I stood frozen in the middle of a grocery store aisle, my eyes glazed over a multitude of cereal brands before they started to well. If you've ever seen the movie *Moscow on the Hudson*, you'll recall a similar scene where Robin Williams's character, who recently defected from Russia, passes out in a grocery store aisle, overwhelmed by the array of choices. To this day, I still get choked up whenever I think about my reaction to the insane abundance of food in our country. We have so much while the world has so little. That lesson never dies.

It reminds me of a black-and-white Peace Corps poster I bought decades ago. In the center is an altered image of Lady Liberty pointing away from Staten Island. Beneath, the caption reads, "Do America a Favor, Leave the Country." For the longest time, I couldn't quite grasp its meaning. But I've long since figured it out.

If I hadn't left the United States to taste what the world has to offer, my world would've remained very small. In turn, my family, friends, and coworkers would never have learned about a gracious people from an African country the size of Maryland. For example, my mother now has something in common with the Ghanaian staff at her retirement community.

In sum, the more we learn about each other, the less we have to fear. The less we fear, the more we're empowered to enjoy and empathize with people from around the globe. Ultimately, our humanity is heightened, ideally making us less inclined to go to war.

It wasn't just Ghanaians who taught me about life, but other foreign nationals I met during my service. While living in the port city of Tema, I met Lebanese, Cubans, Australians, Palestinians, and Egyptians, all of whom opened my eyes to new customs and ways of thinking while revealing my own ignorance about the rest of the world. Over and over, I was shocked to discover how much they knew about my country and how little I knew of theirs. Through countless conversations and heated debates, I vowed never again to be an ignorant American.

In addition to learning from others, I tasted real hardship for the first time in my life. Whether it was food shortages, isolation, or strenuous physical challenges, hardship revealed my capacity for endurance and ingenuity. I simply learned to make do. In the process, I developed an appreciation not only for luxuries taken for granted but the basic necessities of life and their many simple pleasures, including the benefits of physically pushing my boundaries.

From these experiences, my curiosity about other ways of living and thinking only grew. In turn, my perception of choices expanded, as did my comfort level with foreign people and places. This is the very gift I tried to bestow upon my students—the children of migrant workers in Alamosa, Colorado. By helping them look past the wall of societally imposed limitations, my hope was that these kids would discover new horizons affording them more choices in life. In the end, the Universe paid it forward to me.

Ghana bestowed many gifts on me, including new ways of living. To this day, I still opt for candlelight over electricity; manual labor over gadgets; walking over driving; substantive over artificial conversation; and taking the time to scratch out a meal versus popping processed food in the microwave or oven.

Not only did I co-opt new customs, but I developed a whole new level of confidence from debating with Peace Corps volunteers whose education far surpassed mine. After many late-night conversations, it soon became clear I could hold my own. This was among the greatest gifts I brought back from Ghana. Bolstered by a newfound confidence, I returned to college, scored straight A's for the first time in my life, and aced an entrance exam at a private school in Boston, leading to a degree in international relations. Next to joining the Peace Corps, it was the second-best thing I ever did for myself.

Looking back on the trajectory my life has taken since returning from Ghana, it's clear my experience as a Peace Corps volunteer awakened in me a willingness to take risks. I broke through professional barriers that kept me pigeonholed as a legal secretary; I became a freelance writer and moved to Oregon where I worked as a copywriter; then I reinvented my career as a Web content writer and editor in Washington, DC. Throughout this time, I continued volunteering for nonprofit organizations, hosting a Ghanaian exchange student, working with at-risk youth, and helping an Afghan family assimilate to their new life in the United States.

Now here I am living in Jalisco, Mexico, where life is strangely similar to the one I left in Ghana. Once again, I'm living in a culture where people spend much of their time outdoors; where friends and strangers greet each other morning, noon, and night, laughing easily as they prioritize family and community over work; and where the locals teach us gringos to leave behind our hurried ways, yielding to humans over phones. It is a culture that inspires me to give back. In fact, recently, I volunteered as an English teacher for the first time since leaving Ghana.

My life has, indeed, come full circle. And for that I must say, thank you, Ghana. *Medaase paa.*

ACKNOWLEDGMENTS

Many thanks to my mother, Joanne Colbert, for saving my letters from Ghana and for always encouraging me to write; to my father, Chuck Colbert, for fostering my curiosity about the world; to my mentor and friend, Elaine Hagopian, for helping me see culture through a different lens; to my prima, Noelle O'Rourke, for your generous ear and support; to my soulmate in crime, Robin Munroe, for sharing the ride; to my Ghanaian sisters, Pat and Ruby Lamptey, for your friendship and insights; and to my darlin', Richard, for your love and patience. Thank you for encouraging me to put this baby to bed. Last but not least, thank you to my editor, Sally Asante, for your words of wisdom.